The (Un)Welcome Stranger

ALSO BY JEFF MORGAN
AND FROM MCFARLAND

---

*American Comic Poetry: History, Techniques
and Modern Masters* (2015)

The (Un)Welcome Stranger

*Intercultural Sensitivity
in Six American Novels*

JEFF MORGAN

McFarland & Company, Inc., Publishers
Jefferson, North Carolina

This book has undergone peer review.

ISBN (print) 978-1-4766-8565-6
ISBN (ebook) 978-1-4766-4885-9

Library of Congress and British Library
Cataloguing data are available

Library of Congress Control Number 2022055341

Front cover image © 2023 Shutterstock

Printed in the United States of America

*McFarland & Company, Inc., Publishers
Box 611, Jefferson, North Carolina 28640
www.mcfarlandpub.com*

To my son,
Colin Thomas Morgan

Acknowledgments

I would like to thank the following individuals without whom I would have never completed this book: Diane Allerdyce, Milton J. Bennett, Tara Catao, Jordan Chussler, Brit Courtney, John Daily, Otto von Feigenblatt, Lizbeth Keiely, Sheila Sheppard, Rory Spearing, Jared Wellman, Brian J. Whalen, and my wife, Dana Lodge, and my son, Colin Morgan.

Additionally, I would like to thank Lynn University for providing the funding so that I could test this analysis out at conferences, two of which were sponsored by Common Ground.

I am also thankful to the following journals for publishing my work in this area: *Frontiers: The Interdisciplinary Journal of Study Abroad* and *Journal of Alternative Perspectives in the Social Sciences*.

Furthermore, I give thanks to the staffs at the Lynn University Library and Florida Atlantic University's Wimberly Library.

Finally, I'm thankful for my editor, Gary Mitchem, at McFarland.

Table of Contents

Table of Contents

Preface

When I was first exposed to study-abroad theory during a professional development session—presented by Sheila Sheppard at Lynn University in Boca Raton, Florida, where I have taught since the last millennium—I was instantly struck by the literary potential with Milton J. Bennett's Developmental Model of Intercultural Sensitivity.

I at first saw it in the great amount of Florida literature I had been reading. Particularly, Russell Banks' *Continental Drift* and Carl Hiaasen's *Tourist Season*, both set in Florida, seemed to me illustrative of liminality and sensitivity to difference with characters struggling with ethnocentric conflicts and realizing ethnorelative climaxes. Then, I began to see similar ideas in the poetry of Florida poet Campbell McGrath, especially in his *Florida Poems.*

Before long, I expanded my work on this subject. I was presenting at conferences on this and, not long later, publishing on it. I was designing English courses focusing on sensitivity theory and ultimately led a study-abroad program that put into practice my work with using literature to advance sensitivity to difference. We read and studied Ernest Hemingway's novels set in Cuba before spending a week in Cuba ourselves, soaking up as much culture as we could, especially Hemingway's Cuba.

Preface

I had another book project I had already been knee-deep in when these events occurred. When I finished that book in 2015, I began working on this one, bringing in much of what I had learned earlier and adding a lot of what I have learned since. It has been a labor of love.

Everyone gives the name of barbarism to whatever he's unaccustomed to; just as, in reality, it seems we have no other gauge of truth and reasonableness than the example and notion of the opinions and customs of the land we live in.

—Michel de Montainge

Introduction

The (Un)Welcome Stranger is an exploration of the possibilities of intercultural training through literature. To promote understanding across cultural contexts and facilitate communicative competence and intercultural sensitivity, the book will present a behavioral analysis of characters in great American novels. A very useful tool exists with which to accomplish this: Milton J. Bennett's Developmental Model of Intercultural Sensitivity or DMIS, a model of six stages of behavior measuring sensitivity to difference that develops from three initial stages of ethnocentrism to three stages of ethnorelativism. In the latest 2013 edition of his *Basic Concepts of Intercultural Communication*, Bennett writes, "language encourages habitual patterns of perception" (36). These patterns are something characters and narrators disclose, revealing such observable action as conflict due to differing realities colliding between characters, and it can be measured through the systems-based research foundation of the DMIS. In general, the ethnocentric stages characterize individuals whose beliefs and behaviors culled from their primary socialization group remain unquestioned while the ethnorelative stages reveal characters who have recognized that the same beliefs and behaviors are only one organized way of perceiving reality. Using the stages of the DMIS, one can locate characters in literature along the continuum of Bennett's model and analyze their progress. For those in intercultural training and for those who simply love literature, its power to transform readers, and may be themselves interested in becoming more sensitive to difference, this book is dedicated to you. The application of Bennett's model to six novels makes the novels models for a better understanding of where characters, and even the reader, may be on the road to ethnorelativism.

Bennett thoroughly presents the model in his 2004 essay "Becoming Interculturally Competent," and the journey can begin with a simple goal, facilitating initial recognition of difference. Bennett's first stage of the DMIS is called Denial. Here, the characters in the novels will avoid cultural difference. Bennett writes in the essay, "other cultures [are] not noticed" or "vaguely conceived"; other characters are perceived as an "undifferentiated other" by this character who "may act aggressively to avoid or eliminate difference" (63). Before addressing denial, one must become self-aware of where they are in the DMIS, and this book facilitates recognition of place in the process with characters in novels, though this process is not limited to the fiction on these pages. In reality, to prepare for a cross-cultural experience, a facilitator may expose someone who is in Bennett's denial stage to things from a different culture that the person may like, such as food, music, and clothes. Stories can work, too. We can focus on characters who prefer a kind of sameness running into conflict with difference between themselves and another. When a character in denial perceives a kind of personhood in the other, the character in denial is ready to move on to the next stage in Bennett's continuum.

The next stage is Defense. Here, one's own culture is deemed by the character to be the only viable one. Others who are different are often stereotyped. More than once in denial, the character in the stage of defense may act aggressively to avoid or eliminate difference due to feeling more threatened since the different other is more real and may even be thought of as attacking in some way. In the literature, this character's conflict will involve stereotyping and criticizing difference. When the character in defense perceives common ground with a different other, a mutual dependence can be created, although in "Becoming Interculturally Competent," Bennett warns of Reversal, "a variation on defense [that] may masquerade as cultural sensitivity" (66). Wary of reversal, the character whose climax involves the perception of common ground seems prepared to proceed to the next stage of Bennett's DMIS.

The last of Bennett's ethnocentric stops along the continuum of the DMIS is Minimization. Now, the character may trivialize another culture. In the novels, this character, when confronted with one who has a different cultural worldview, will focus on the sameness between them as if to say "You know what I like about you? The part of you that's like me." As Bennett writes, one is experiencing "elements of one's own cultural worldview ... as universal" (66–67). This character could easily slide back into the defense stage. Bennett accounts for relapses. What this character needs to do to become more interculturally sensitive is reconcile unity and diversity, accept the common humanity as well as that which makes us different. The character should focus more on difference to progress through the continuum of the DMIS, and when the character does seem to climactically perceive both unity and diversity, that character appears ready to move into the ethnorelative stages of Bennett's model.

The first is Acceptance, which does not mean agreement. The danger here can be for one to accept that which perhaps ought not to be accepted, similar to a relativism in which it's all good. This can lead to characters struggling with relativity and ethics. Still, more positively speaking, this character in the literature will note others are different, equally important, and human. With a literary study, we can focus on characters because they are, as Bennett writes in *Basic Concepts of Intercultural Communication*, "individuals [who] manifest culture through their worldviews" and who manifest intercultural sensitivity "by a predominant experience of difference" (85), a conflict in other words. This intercultural sensitivity, along with the character being negatively judgmental concerning some things about those who are culturally different, points to progress along the DMIS. The character accepts much about the different other, but not everything. The next thing you know, this character may start putting some of those new worldviews into practice.

A character behaving this way and revealing intercultural

sensitivity signals the next step as we progress through the DMIS: Adaptation. Due to the accepting nature of the character progressing thus, Bennett describes this character now as one whose "worldview [will be] expanded to include relevant constructs from other cultural worldviews" (70), leading potentially to empathy and becoming the basis for bi- or multiculturality that is unlike assimilation or melting pot thinking in that it involves expansion, leading one to define oneself more broadly. In the novels, we will be looking for characters whose adaptation is exemplified through modification of behavior, change, probably climactic, exemplifying the emergence of an alternative worldview. The DMIS measures the adaptation while the novel serves as the empirical field observation. The formal elements of literature serve as the neutral criteria. What we want to keep a keen eye out for is the character being authentic, that this behavior is not just some cultural appropriation.

In the final step of the DMIS, Integration, a character may have so adapted one or more cultural worldviews that the character can be like one from a different culture, and almost blend in. Bennett used to refer to this type of individual as a constructive marginal but has since turned to liminality to try to characterize such a character. Liminality is less negative to be sure, for it simply suggests an expansion of worldviews that allows one to move in and out of cultures. Now Bennett views marginality as something to be avoided. The analysis of these characters in American novels will lead to perceiving some characters who are integrating as liminal though they may appear marginalized. For instance, Ishmael in Herman Melville's *Moby-Dick* and the nameless narrator of Ralph Ellison's *Invisible Man* are both seemingly separated from others at the end of their respective narratives; however, each also writes his book, which is his way of reaching out from the separation and, through liminality, connects with a rainbow coalition of readers.

Bennett's switch to liminality as more appropriate terminology has its roots in the works of ethnographer and folklorist Arnold Van Gennep from the early twentieth century and Victor Turner, an anthropologist from the 1960s. Van Gennep's *The Rites of Passage* from 1960 sets the stage for Bennett's DMIS with his three-phase process toward a liminal mind (11). His first stage is pre-liminal and involves rites of separation. The characters in these six novels each experience an early separation. Ishmael leaves land for a whaling adventure in Melville's *Moby-Dick.* Hester is forced to live on the outskirts of town in Nathaniel Hawthorne's *The Scarlet Letter.* Sarah Orne Jewett's nameless narrator of *The Country of the Pointed Firs* leaves the city for the country. The American in Henry James' *The American* leaves America for Europe. Ellison's nameless narrator of *Invisible Man* finds himself experiencing a series of separations, starting at college, and Ernest Hemingway's Robert Jordan in *For Whom the Bell Tolls* has left his Montana teaching position to fight in the Spanish Civil War. The separation for each character puts them into conflicts in which they must relate to different worldviews, and we can measure their actions using Bennett's DMIS.

After the separation, Van Gennep has two more stages. He would describe the next action in these narratives as transition rites, transition into liminality. For Van Gennep, the transitioning is like being in a neutral zone (18). He also suggests some marginality with transitioning in that the character in the novel would be "isolated and maintained in an intermediate position" (186). We will see all of our main characters in these six novels transition except for Newman in *The American.* It is a satire after all. So, Newman never really experiences any rites of incorporation, what Van Gennep would describe as a post-liminal time. James' great novel is in here on the grounds that sometimes it is best to understand something by what it is not. In spiritual terms, Van Gennep's relational process works like an individual beginning work with a guru, learning from the guru, and ultimately attaining oneness. Imagine everyone attaining oneness. Imagine everyone attaining liminality. No wonder Victor Turner praises a hippie world (112) in his influential *The Ritual Process* from 1969.

Turner's book also influences Bennett's DMIS and this literary analysis. In the novels in this analysis, liminal characters will at times experience conflict because of their liminality when they find themselves in a one-sided ethnocentric society. For instance, Hester,

Introduction

in Hawthorne's *The Scarlet Letter*, seems to have attained a kind of liminality, a binary, dual, two-sided one in this case, and she is ostracized by a community of one-sided people. Ellison's nameless narrator in *Invisible Man* may carry off the point best of all. Turner notes a linkage of the liminal to the marginal character and further notes an inferiority with the liminal or marginal character even though that character is more open (110). The reader is left to imagine how Melville's Ishmael or Jewett's nameless narrator will deal with their liminality as those novels end before they can take their newfound liminality into another worldview. Hemingway's Jordan dies at the end of his novel, and *The American* is a satire of the process of attaining sensitivity to difference, the movement from ethnocentric behavior to ethnorelative behavior, the reaching of liminality, leaving those texts out of this particular conflict. We see how Bennett is standing on Turner's shoulders. I am, too. Turner also writes that art or literature in a liminal vein often has "a multivocal character, having many meanings, and each is capable of moving people at many psychological levels simultaneously" (129). In addition to Ellison's nameless narrator coming to mind, there is this book, examining six American novels from different eras and a veritable cornucopia of worldviews to analyze.

The analysis will be formal, a New Critical approach, which is now an old approach, but it might be the closest thing we have to a paradigm in literary theory. One must start somewhere, and the formal elements can be agreed upon. Two of the most basic components of plot structure are conflict and climax. In this book, the conflicts will be seen to be cross-cultural, while the climaxes will tend to be intercultural. Conflict occurs through contact by a less sensitive, more ethnocentric character with one culturally different, a clash between worldviews. Bennett writes in *Basic Concepts* that conflicts are "created from differently contexted experience" (38). The climax leaves us with a changed character who is interculturally sensitive. This book will "focus on characters because they are individuals [who] manifest culture through their worldviews" and who manifest intercultural sensitivity "by a predominant experience of difference" (85). A systematic observation of characters in American novels will show that experience is constructed and that people can become more, or less, sensitive to cultural difference.

That's why this book is a developmental intervention. A reader will likely enhance intercultural sensitivity simply by exposure to how the process of moving from ethnocentrism to ethnorelativism plays out in the novels. As society becomes more pluralistic, studies involving sensitivity to difference are needed. Could such studies having a literary approach have an effect and do something like stop White flight or stereotyping? If this book had any effect on a reader, the objective would be as bold in this book as in any intercultural training. As Bennett writes, the goal is "to overcome ethnocentrism and to enable successful interaction in a multicultural environment," perhaps even enabling one "to transcend [one's] own limited experience and imagine the world as another is experiencing it" (49). This study delivers that. This study simply uses cross-cultural contact by characters in American novels to chart their movement along Bennett's DMIS and enhance intercultural learning, which "contributes to intercultural competence and thus to global citizenship" (111). At the very least, *The (Un)Welcome Stranger* enhances intercultural sensitivity, the perception of cultural difference, and that is the starting point before any intercultural learning can take place, let alone any sensitivity leading to behavior modification in another cultural context.

Literary theory furthers this view. For example, Wolfgang Iser discussed how literature can help us better understand ourselves, our values or the codes we live by. We can be transformed. The transformation can come from codes transferred from different cultures through literature. When reading about one who is culturally different from myself, I learn that character's customary codes unless, as Terry Eagleton emphasizes with Iser, we have "a reader with strong ideological commitments" (79). That reader will be less likely to transform. So, as long as the reader is open, a theorist such as Louis Althusser would argue that a societal ideology can be transmitted from literature, molding and shaping readers. One could argue, for instance, that the phallogocentric style dominates the western world, molding and shaping individuals and groups. I am thinking of Gloria

Introduction

Steinem's brilliant landing to her 1970 Senate testimony in favor of the Equal Rights Amendment (ERA). She closes with "after all, we won't have our masculinity to prove" (para. 33). She is clearly suggesting the different worldview of giving women more power might be a good thing. More worldviews are a good thing.

Yes, literary theory can help us address how to better relate, and intercultural sensitivity research has proven time and again that Bennett's DMIS is a strong model for almost thirty years. In a 2003 article in *The International Journal of Intercultural Relations*, R. Michael Paige and others analyze a new model, co-created by Bennett, called the Intercultural Development Inventory (IDI). It is based on Bennett's old model. The IDI suggests different stages of development but is so similar to the DMIS that the research shows the strength of Bennett's DMIS. Nothing better has come down the pike. To be sure, in a 2019 article published in *Global Education Review*, an article about promoting intercultural competence, McGregor et al. write, "The Developmental Model of Intercultural Sensitivity (DMIS) provided the conceptual frame for this study—offering the operational definition of intercultural competence—specifically framing one's orientation towards cultural difference" (44). Bennett's DMIS will be the scale by which the following analysis will determine whether, for example, a certain character's words and actions are relational, sensitive, and civil, or non-relational, insensitive, and uncivil. Let us begin.

ONE

The Nineteenth Century Romantic Novel

Moby-Dick and *The Scarlet Letter*

1

Melville's Liminal One

Ishmael and the Developmental Model
of Intercultural Sensitivity

Others have analyzed the character of Ishmael within a context of intercultural sensitivity. Melville clearly aligns Ishmael with Jonah, inviting criticism based on the allusion, but more to the point, in his landmark *American Renaissance: Art and Expression in the Age of Emerson and Whitman* (1941), F.O. Matthiessen discusses the runaway nature of Ishmael's character. He characterizes Ishmael as, at least early on in the novel, an existentialist in the sense, particularly, of "an individual's separation from his fellow human beings" (443). In this sense, Melville is prescient regarding the dilemma of the modern man in much of twentieth-century American literature. For Matthiessen, Ishmael's sensitivity conflict, his isolation, climaxes still early in the novel with Queequeg. "When Ishmael recognized that 'the man's a human being just as I am,' he was freed from the burden of his isolation, his heart was no longer turned against society" (443). Analyzing Matthiessen's reading of the conflict and climax of Ishmael's meeting with Queequeg within a framework of intercultural sensitivity reveals the basic truths of Bennett's intercultural sensitivity model as Ishmael moves from ethnocentric to ethnorelative behavior, primarily because he shared a bed with a presumed savage, a predominant experience and a strong representation of integration, the final phase in Bennett's model.

However, by the end of the novel Ishmael becomes a constructive marginal, and, still, this is an area Matthiessen explores. He addresses Ishmael's multiple perspectives in Melville's chapter 42, "The Whiteness of the Whale." Ishmael's willingness to accept multiple interpretations of the symbolism of the color white follows two chapters in which Melville suggests the need for intercultural sensitivity. In chapter 40, Melville gives a good idea of how multicultural the *Pequod* is; not all the crew equally appreciates some of the singing and dancing, and there is almost a battle royale at the end. These individuals clearly need to be more accepting of difference. Then, Melville characterizes Ishmael as one who can read a symbol more than one way and abide by its hidden truths though, namely here with the whale, he reads dark portents. Here, he is not unlike Hamlet, who has given himself to providence. Ishmael abides by the majority opinion, confessing "I gave myself up to the abandonment of the time and the place; but while yet all a-rush to encounter the whale, could see naught in that brute but the deadliest ill" (203). An activist would have Ishmael intervene, but Ishmael is not an activist; he is, as Bennett wrote in 1993, a constructive marginal, constantly creating his own reality (M. Bennett 64), a reality that Janet Bennett characterizes as "commitment in relativism" (117) and which Matthiessen pegs decades before when he recognizes that the "one thing that could redeem 'the wolfish world,' the Ishmael of *Moby-Dick* found, was sympathy with another human being" (443). That drive for connection will manifest itself in his writing, for, as the narrator of *Moby-Dick*, he exhibits, similar to Ellison's nameless narrator in *Invisible Man*, liminality and sensitivity to difference, the liminality better fitting a characterization of Ishmael than constructive marginal.

Other great scholars after Matthiessen also characterize Ishmael in terms of intercultural sensitivity but without the context of intercultural sensitivity theory woven into their analyses; however, it is there in spirit. It is there when Richard Chase in his significant book from 1957, *The American Novel and Its Tradition*, writes about Ishmael looking into the water. Unlike Ahab, Ishmael, as Chase points out, sees his "own image in a context of life and reality" (108). In terms of intercultural sensitivity theory, Chase's contrast is clear, for Ahab is the poster child for ethnocentric behavior, his condition, in fact, frequently referred to as monomaniacal. Ishmael, on the other hand, views himself in a context. Leslie Fiedler, three years later in his *Love and Death in the American Novel*, further underlines the importance of understanding Ishmael from a standpoint of intercultural sensitivity. Fiedler focuses on Ishmael's relationship with Queequeg and is quick to draw attention to Ishmael's intercultural insensitivity early in the novel. "Everything about Queequeg appalls him," but in a short time, "he awakens in the harpooner's embrace" (534). Queequeg's tomahawk pipe becomes a peace pipe, and Queequeg's idol, Yojo, becomes the recipient of repeated ritualistic condescension from Ishmael. Fiedler also marks Ishmael's relapses, as with Elijah after Ishmael and Queequeg sign on with the *Pequod*, or when Ishmael "lent his voice to the pledge of the maddened crew to pursue the abominable quest" (550). In his most recent edition of *Basic Concepts*, Bennett explains setbacks or relapses along the developmental process, writing "unresolved issues from earlier stages can become problems later" (87). Ultimately, Fiedler, too, recognizes Ishmael's ethnorelativism, turning to "The Monkey Rope" chapter of the novel to help symbolize integration and the "A Squeeze of the Hand" chapter to epitomize integration with Ishmael asserting, "nay, let us all squeeze ourselves into each other; let us squeeze ourselves universally into the very milk and sperm of kindness" (456).

Since these pioneering works on American literature, a plethora of books have added to the analysis of Ishmael as a liminal character who goes through the process of intercultural sensitivity. The same year Criterion brought out Fiedler's fresh views of Ishmael and Queequeg's relationship, Merlin Brown's *The Long Encounter: Self and Experience in the Writings of Herman Melville* came out. Brown, though, writes "we must not expect an exact sequence of steps" charting Ishmael's growth of intercultural sensitivity (241).

With Bennett's DMIS, now we can. This is why this time spent on Ishmael is important, for Melville's character may be one of the best in American literature to illustrate the scope of Bennett's model. In 1973, others, including Robert Zoellner, continued looking for a process, a model, within which the growth of Ishmael's character could be better explained, and Zoellner notes Ishmael's view of the whale moves from demonic monster to fish to mammal to brother (185). In his 1991 book, *The Machine in the Garden,* Leo Marx asserts how Ishmael, after surviving the adventure of the *Pequod,* develops a narrative voice that embraces two distinct voices, "the claims of our collective, institutional life and the claims of nature" (285). In the 1980s and 1990s, writers such as Robert Martin and William V. Spanos, in other large works on Melville, analyze Ishmael in economic terms addressing two sides to Ishmael's character, the individual who leads to imperialism and the more liminal type of characterization that leads to a more liberating multiplicity. To be sure, Nina Baym, John Bryant, and Lawrence Buell all address "Melville's complex marginalizing rhetoric" (Bryant 708), but, again, it is important to remember that Ishmael is not marginalized for long. He ultimately writes *Moby-Dick,* connecting to the world and connecting the world.

In the past half century, several articles have appeared addressing the issue of Ishmael's character and liminality. In 1967, David Hirsch writes briefly in *AN&Q,* "Ishmael actually presents himself in two guises in the novel" (115). Melville, though, does not stop the multiple layers of Ishmael's liminal characterization at two. Three fine essays on the subject of multiplicity come out in the 1980s. Philip Egan's "Time and Ishmael's Character in 'The Town-Ho's Story' of *Moby-Dick*" focuses on the story within the story to assert Ishmael's discomfort with his audience and pinpoints his growth toward liminality at some mid-point; however, Egan writes, "we cannot refer to *Moby-Dick* as a bildungsroman or 'novel of education' because we do not really know the stages and methods by which Ishmael achieves his growth" (338). This, you see, is where Milton Bennett's DMIS helps. Mark Patterson, in a 1984 writing, anticipates Ishmael's remarkable growth and analyzes a process but doesn't go all the way with Ishmael, relegating his development in a tone of loss when he writes that Ishmael's "voice later seems to disappear into the narrative itself, mimicking a variety of other voices as the novel progresses" (297). The disappearance he refers to is actually Ishmael's new character, the liminality, the rainbow coalition of cultural influences. In 1989, Susan Lyne Knutson clearly brings the discussion into the context of intercultural sensitivity studies when she analyzes "Wheelbarrow," chapter 13 in the novel, in which Queequeg turns cultural tables on Ishmael, pointing out the difficulties one has grasping customs when in a different culture and how the natives are inclined to be derisive. Knutson claims the passage "indicates that Melville was aware of the problems with ethnocentric vision, and was perhaps as conscious of them as a man of his time might be" (par. 27).

More recently, the critical analysis seems to be even more closely following Bennett's stages. Robert Martin returns to the subject in a smart 1990 essay, "Sleeping with a Savage: Deculturation in *Moby-Dick*," in which he asserts Ishmael's ethnocentric character early in the novel is the result of cultural homophobic conditioning. He recognizes that Melville clearly juxtaposes Queequeg's Yojo with Father Mapple's Christ to illustrate the existence of different visions, and recognizes different voices in Ishmael, noting, at least three. Joseph Adriano's "Brother to Dragons: Race and Evolution in *Moby-Dick*," from 1996, points to Melville's thematic tendency to undercut traditional hierarchies, which echoes the work of intercultural sensitivity scholars who point to the traveler abroad who now prefers abroad to the United States, a clear example of Bennett's reversal. Adriano, though, takes Ishmael's character even farther down the line of Bennett's intercultural sensitivity development, characterizing Ishmael as too smart to fight the Leviathan; instead, he embraces it, just as he embraces the harpooners who also embrace the Leviathan. This is the community of liminality. Recent ecocriticism, a field closely related to intercultural sensitivity, by Elizabeth Schultz and Susan Kalter expand that community to include the whale. Schultz focuses on "cetacean and human kinship" (104) that recalls Bennett's stage of minimization in the way that Ishmael admires the human qualities in the whale. Kalter writes of savagism in whale hunting, which closely resembles Bennett's ethnocentrism. "Melville's radical ecology," to Kalter, further connects "to the valuing of Native American cultures" (13). Still furthering the community, Thomas L. Dumm, in a 2005 essay, expands it to include the reader. Dumm characterizes readers of the novel as fellow liminal ones, and Ishmael asking to be named at the beginning of the novel can be seen as an effort toward a union of isolatoes (400) or fellow "liminars," bringing the reader into the discussion.

Let us now turn to the text for a close reading and analyze this process of Ishmael's growth toward becoming liminal, and there is no better place to start than the beginning. We have already seen how Robert Martin suggests cultural conditioning has gone into Ishmael's character even before the curtain rises on *Moby-Dick*. Before the action starts at the Spouter Inn, Melville tells us a lot about Ishmael. He can tell a story, which is no small feat; however, despite this skill, Ishmael is poor, disinterested with society, grim, of a damp and drizzly soul, fixated on death, and ready for violence. He also needs to get to water to best reflect. Ishmael minimalizes cultural difference when he lumps everyone with himself as "tied … nailed … [and] clinched" (4), and he exhibits similar ethnocentric behavior when he heralds the universal appeal of water for purposes of reflection. Further minimization occurs when Ishmael places everyone on the stage, the play being the thing that providentially unites us. Early in the novel, Ishmael trivializes difference, exhibiting what Milton Bennett characterizes in "Towards Ethnorelativism," from Michael Paige's 1993 anthology of essays on intercultural sensitivity, as transcendent universalism since Ishmael seems to have fallen for the single truth fallacy (41–44).

Once Melville takes the action to the Spouter Inn, which represents worldliness due to its diverse clientele, Ishmael's ethnocentrism takes center stage. A potential conflict arises because Ishmael must share a bed with another man, Queequeg, but Ishmael has not seen the harpooner. Our hero claims, "I would put up with the half of any decent man's blanket" (15). The key word there is the adjective *decent*. Ishmael begins "to feel suspicious of this 'dark complexioned harpooner'" whose bed he is to share. He even associates the harpooner with the Devil and assumes a position of superiority over the man he is supposed to sleep with, thinking the harpooner "must undress and get into bed" (16) first. Ishmael would clearly be more comfortable sleeping with a man more like himself, like Bulkington, aloof, alone. Ishmael's anxiety with strangeness is classic defense behavior in intercultural sensitivity theory. He is experiencing a cultural conflict (Wurzel 6–7), and it is a great conflict or predominant experience for our purposes because the harpooner is so different than Ishmael. As Paige points out, the greater the cultural difference, the greater the challenge ("On the Nature" 5).

Ishmael appears to have skipped Bennett's first stage of cultural sensitivity, denial. Bennett characterizes, in part, the first phase of this ethnocentric behavior as isolation, a trait, despite what Matthiessen writes, seemingly not on Ishmael's person. A teacher who chooses to get away from it all by boarding a whaler that symbolically represents the world, Ishmael is aware of cultural difference. He does not choose separation, another of Bennett's defining characteristics of the defense stage. Boarding the *Pequod*, a whaling vessel certainly with a motley crew, symbolically suggests Ishmael is actually embracing the world. Ishmael does, though, get a little defensive about cultural difference, as we have seen above. Ishmael exhibits the three main characteristics about defense. He denigrates the harpooner when associating him with the Devil. He also shows his sense of superiority over the harpooner with his condescending tone when describing Queequeg's ritual with his idol. Not long after the episode at the Spouter Inn, Ishmael even begins Bennett's final phase of defense, reversal, in which the ethnocentric person denies his previous superiority and acknowledges his own inferiority in the sense that the character seems to prefer the newly exposed to different cultural worldview. Though Ishmael seems to skip the stage of denial, he definitely exhibits behavior characteristic of Bennett's second stage, defense. Ishmael will proceed through the other stages of Bennett's Developmental Model of Intercultural Sensitivity, and he will experience relapses along the way; however, within the Spouter Inn episode, Melville packs a boatload of details that lend themselves to looking at his novel through the lens of intercultural sensitivity theory.

A brief look at some other key action under the roof of the Spouter Inn reveals how significant the episode is in establishing Ishmael's course through the stages of cultural sensitivity, starting with defense. He does accept to share a bed with Queequeg, but only after it appears Queequeg isn't returning to the inn. He tries on Queequeg's poncho-mat, but, seeing his reflection, freaks out, and disrobes. Certain that his roommate is an evil killer, Ishmael commends himself "to care of heaven" (22). Once Ishmael finally sees Queequeg's face, he revolts. Ishmael seems to want to accept Queequeg, but his fears result in Ishmael virtually denying Queequeg's existence by remaining silent and pretending not to be there in bed. Once the two are aware of the other's existence, an apparent murder ends with Ishmael admiring Queequeg's simple integrity, which suggests Bennett's idea of reversal, but he minimizes Queequeg when he says, "the man's a human being just as I am" (26). This is very limited acceptance and overall behavior primarily indicative of Bennett's defensive stage. After all, as the episode comes to a close, Ishmael demands that Queequeg adapt to Ishmael's ways, and Queequeg, seemingly beyond Ishmael when it comes to accepting difference, does so willingly. Still, at the very end of the episode, and suggestive that Ishmael will progress through further stages of cultural sensitivity, we have the positive sign of Ishmael sleeping his best sleep ever.

Life with Queequeg after that first night at the Spouter Inn continues to conflict Ishmael as he struggles with his own ethnocentric side. Melville's symbols, such as their embrace, the patchwork quilt, Queequeg's tattoos, and the blending of the latter two, represent cultural integration, but soon give way to more ethnocentric detailing. For example, Ishmael starts to see Queequeg as superior in a bit of reversal, but soon reverts back to a standard culturally defensive posture. He adopts a defensive tone in "The Street," chapter six, associating Queequeg with diction such as "outlandish" and "wild" and "cannibals" and "savages" (36). Melville also mixes in more ethnorelative detailing as Ishmael accepts Queequeg's harpoon as a razor and an eating utensil. There is a lot that Ishmael can learn about intercultural sensitivity from Queequeg, especially from the way the harpooner adapts to boots, but an even stronger teaching moment occurs when Ishmael sees Queequeg at the Whaleman's Chapel. After the Spouter Inn episode, Ishmael is well on his way toward becoming a more liminal character, but Queequeg appears to be already there. Again, by these terms, Bennett, in "Becoming Interculturally Competent," seems to describe a character such as Ishmael is becoming as "maybe at the margins of two or more cultures and central to none" (72). This could lead to alienation or a more positive constructive marginality or multiculturalism as Bennett has more recently written regarding liminality.

Now, here at this chapel, Melville provides significant detailing that needs to be viewed with a culturally sensitive gaze. For years, sailors from around the world have found themselves in New Bedford and the Whaleman's Chapel, each needing to adapt to certain things in these settings, so Ishmael's visit to the house of worship definitely suggests he's integrating. Particularly, Father Mapple's sermon is instructive. Stylistically, the sermon is important in terms of intercultural sensitivity because it is the first extended speech from someone other than Ishmael and subsequently advances Melville's theme involving multiplicity and ambiguity. Furthermore, the actual content of Father Mapple's sermon also enhances intercultural sensitivity. The preacher asks his parishioners to sacrifice what they want to do in order to follow another, in this case, God. This is the story of Jonah, and this is not unlike Queequeg's sacrifice with the boots.

After church, the chapters leading up to the disembarking of the *Pequod* further Ishmael's education, albeit in a rather wavering way. Ishmael reverts to a defensive tone with diction such as "heathenish," "savage," and "hideously marred" (55), referring to Queequeg's tattoos. But, he adds, "Through all his unearthly tattooings, I thought I saw the traces of a simple honest heart" (55). This acceptance, which is Bennett's fourth stage and first of three in the ethnorelative stages, continues for a page in the novel until a minimization snag occurs with some reversal, both indicative of Ishmael backsliding to ethnocentric stages. Ishmael minimizes Queequeg by suggesting that one thing he likes about the harpooner is his phrenological resemblance to George Washington, a comparison that also reveals

Ishmael's admiration for Queequeg, but only in a limited worldview. More of the same can be seen a bit later when Ishmael sees the wisdom in adopting some of Queequeg's way of looking at the world, mainly indifferent that is, and in spending a second night together. Along the way, they share a pipe, symbolic of their integration, which Queequeg takes a step farther with more physical connection that represents a bosom friendship and even marriage. At the same time Ishmael behaves in a more ethnocentric way with lines such as "I'll try a pagan friend thought I, since Christian kindness has proved but hollow courtesy" (57), clearly exemplifying Bennett's reversal description. This jagged process leading to Ishmael's liminality is not unprecedented in cultural sensitivity theory. In fact, Kenneth Cushner describes a tension in someone who is attracted to cultural maintenance and to cultural pluralism (353), which can be seen as adding to a repertoire of cultural worldviews, a repertoire that could have any number of additions. In this specific case, when Ishmael refers to Queequeg as a pagan, he would be in the maintenance side of the conflict, and the more open side is evident in the openness to spend a second night with Queequeg. A formal analysis of Ishmael's conflict here clearly can be articulated using intercultural sensitivity theory, which is why anyone could benefit from mapping Ishmael's sojourn of the self.

Still early in the novel, after a few pages dripping with ethnocentrism, Melville again brings up Ishmael's conflict as described by Cushner. Ishmael's biography of Queequeg is especially telling here. The diction mixes words such as "savage" and "wild" and all of their connotative baggage with a more regal tone. This is soon followed by the aforementioned wheelbarrow scene, significant for its lesson that is perhaps best described in Queequeg's words: "It's a mutual, joint-stock world, in all meridians" (68), which alludes to him helping the greenhorn and the captain, who both thought lightly of Queequeg. To be sure, the harpooner serves as a strong role model for Ishmael. Queequeg is eager to integrate, hoping to adapt certain characteristics that he can then take home for his people. He does not overthink situations that could be characterized as predominant experiences. As a model for Ishmael, Queequeg's empathy recalls

Bennett's words from *Basic Concepts*, "the process of intercultural sensitivity from ethnocentrism to ethnorelativism is not predominantly a cerebral one—it is embodied" (44). That is not to say Queequeg followed such a process, but Ishmael must; moreover, he must reach that level of embodying the worldview of a different other as Queequeg does. However, as Melville's narrative is about set to sail, Ishmael still reveals himself as culturally conflicted, unable, for instance, to understand Queequeg's spirituality even though he certainly tries.

The trying shows Ishmael struggling through Bennett's stages, and in the chapters before embarkation, Ishmael reveals himself to still have one foot stepping back into ethnocentrism and the other stepping forward into ethnorelativism. To illustrate, notice Ishmael combines acceptance with defense when he says at the start of chapter 17, "I cherish the greatest respect towards everybody's religious obligations, never mind how comical" (90). The two sides to that quote help show Ishmael has a way to go. In fact, most of Melville's detailing keeps his characterization of Ishmael within ethnocentric parameters. Still, despite all of Ishmael's ethnocentric behavior, referring to Queequeg's Ramadan rituals as intolerable, despite his differences with Queequeg, they saunter off together to the *Pequod*. It is there where Ishmael will continue to grow, referring to life aboard the *Pequod* as his Yale and Harvard.

The whole novel takes a turn once the *Pequod* is off, and intercultural sensitivity seems to take a back seat to other more pressing thematic concerns in Melville's story. Ishmael, indeed, appears to disappear into chapters of unseen predominant experiences. Yet, the whole novel can be seen as maintaining a thematic focus on intercultural sensitivity. Even chapters that focus on other mammals, such as the chapter on cetology, work, as Marx, Schultz, Kalter, and others have pointed out, within a context of intercultural sensitivity theory because Melville, here, forces the reader to change his view of the whale, just as he forces the reader to change with further characterization of Ahab. The infamous captain of the *Pequod* has reached the end of Bennett's process, but Ahab's adaptation of multiple worldviews has melted down into a monomania far from the character comfortably embracing liminality. In "Towards Eth-norelativism," Milton Bennett, in his pre-liminal days, character-izes the constructive marginal as one who is constantly creating his own reality (64). Indeed, Ahab, attaching a high importance to his own opinion, has constructed a reality, fed by his monomania, which perceives the whale, Moby-Dick, as a wall that, if torn down or, killed, will then reveal some hidden truth. Ahab's common char-acterization as a Transcendentalist gone mad, which is one rea-son why Melville is often linked with his mentor Hawthorne as an anti-Transcendentalist, is not all that different, in the end, than Ahab's characterization as a constructive marginal gone mad. As Janet Bennett points out, again in a pre-liminal view, to the construc-tive marginal "ambiguity seems overwhelming" (117), and ambiguity and hidden truth heap Ahab. Ishmael seems to better fit the liminal characterization, but Ahab may better fit the old constructive mar-ginal view.

Another theme that, at first, may seem disconnected with a dis-cussion of intercultural sensitivity theory is Melville's treatment of democracy. In contrast to crews on merchant-marine vessels, which Ishmael has experience on, the *Pequod* is "barbaric, heathenish, and motley" (133). If the *Pequod* represents only the United States and all her cultural diversity, our population, as Melville sees it, appears in a rather dim light. Still, Ishmael talks of the dignity in free democ-racy, praising the common man's potential, which is definitely eth-norelative. Ishmael clearly opposes a pessimistic view of folks when he says, "man, in the ideal, is so noble and so sparkling, such a grand and glowing creature, that over any ignominious blemish in him all of his fellows should run to throw their costliest robes." A sentence later, he adds that the "dignity I treat of, is not the dignity of kings and robes, but that abounding dignity which has no robed investi-ture. Thou shalt see it shining in the arm that wields a pick or drives a spike; that democratic dignity" that Ishmael further character-izes as "centre and circumference of all democracy" (126). The sense of acceptance that resonates in these lines connects with intercul-tural sensitivity theory. By openly embracing all the cultural differ-ence on board the *Pequod*, Ishmael not only promotes democracy. He promotes notions that differences are necessary and preferable, that choices are not based on absolutes (M. Bennett, "Towards Ethnorelativism" 47–48). Certainty, such as Ahab's, can be seen as a detriment to ethnorelativism.

At sea, Melville's characterization of Ishmael still remains in a kind of transitional phase shifting between ethnocentrism and ethnorelativism. Ishmael's word choices can be denigrating, suggesting his sense of cultural superiority when he refers to the "diabolism" in Ahab's special crew, defensive diction that compounds with his characterization of Fedallah's "half-hissed" voice (236). Both examples illustrate Ishmael's sense of evil and the Devil with those in question. This special crew has made its first appearance from below deck upon the first lowering for whales. The response to their appearance from Archy, the one who heard them earlier, helps put Ishmael's intercultural sensitivity in perspective, for Archy seems to accept them. Stubb, too, seems to accept them; however, he does refer to the special crew members as "devils" (237). The rather existential Starbuck accepts Ahab's special crew but refers to their being onboard as "a sad business" (238). Remember, acceptance is not agreement. Ishmael, perhaps less of a businessman, also begins to accept these men, but his sensitivity will go beyond that of any of these other characters. Still, he wavers. Ishmael demonstrates some reversal when he elevates Daggoo above Flask, and his tendency toward minimization reoccurs with his line, "Verily, there is nothing new under the sun" (228), a rather insensitive remark since it posits that there is no cultural difference that Ishmael has not experienced, which is not exactly the most sensitive line coming from one who is to be the heroic liminal one at the end of the narrative. Yet, to Ishmael's credit, his weaving with Queequeg, at least symbolically, not only addresses time, but their collaborative effort points to integration.

Chapter 49, called "The Hyena," may serve as a turning point for Ishmael's progression as, at this point, much more of Melville's detailing going toward characterization of his narrator includes action that suits ethnorelativism a bit more. Here, Ishmael hints at traumatic or predominant experiences as a teacher of acceptance and adaptation. He mentions how life naturally throws these experiences into one's path and how he, particularly, has come to terms with these. For Ishmael, he now realizes "nothing dispirits, and nothing seems worth disputing. He bolts down all events, all creeds, and beliefs, and persuasions" (247). His openness, his willingness to accept and adapt, will become intensified on the *Pequod*, noting that there's "nothing like the perils of whaling to breed this free and easy sort of genial, desperado philosophy" (247). Ishmael is accepting the world outside himself, and Melville's detailing begins to accelerate that notion at this stage in the novel. To be sure, Melville has picked a setting and cast of characters conducive to ethnorelative sentiments because sailors tend to have a range of experience that goes beyond most landlubbers. In chapter 53, "The Gam," Melville clearly asserts this notion about sailors, attributed to shared profession and "common pursuit and mutually shared privations and perils" (261), all of which makes Ishmael becoming liminal aboard the *Pequod* rather moot unless evidence of ethnocentrism is seen onboard.

Fortunately, the very next chapter, "The Town-Ho's Story," helps keep such a conflict front and center in the narrative. Although, Melville takes Ishmael off the ship and to another time to accomplish this. In Lima, Ishmael integrates, but the Peruvians' self-deprecating humor, their anti-Christian comments, and their tendency to minimalize with lines like "the world's one Lima" (274), all help bring out the ethnocentric side of Ishmael. Upon moving his detailing back aboard the *Pequod*, Melville brings Ishmael back to more ethnocentric characterizations. He has Ishmael acting metaphorically defensive when he equates hemp rope with "a dusky, dark fellow, a sort of Indian; but Manilla [rope] is as a golden-haired Circassian to behold" (303). And he shows reversal when he raises a famished Fejee cannibal above the "unlighted gourmand, who nailest geese to the ground and fastest on their bloated livers in thy pate-de-fois-gras" (327). And, yes, even his tone echoes reversal.

Melville perhaps best presents insensitivity to difference on board the *Pequod* when he turns to more commercial or capitalistic detailing. Ishmael feels for the whale. Whales, like the buffalo, seen abstractly as humans, suggest a certain level of denial, the first level of ethnocentrism, through the actual hunting and drastic reduction of their numbers. Stubb evinces just such ethnocentric Capitalism during the Pip episode. He "indirectly hinted, that though man loves his fellow, yet man is a money-making animal, which propensity too often interferes with his benevolence" (452). Stubb also has some strong words for the French. But more to the case, is the fast-fish/loose-fish analogy, which is not from Ishmael's mind but something that he reports on, and it smacks of sexism and nationalism. It is safe to say that Ishmael encounters plenty of ethnocentric behavior aboard the *Pequod*. From the ethnocentricity of Peleg, whom Ishmael encounters as he and Queequeg sign up for their voyage; to both Peleg and Bildad being insensitive to Queequeg, especially Bildad, who tries to convert Queequeg; to the fight aboard ship in chapter 40, a fight that starts because of the cultural insensitivity of a Spanish sailor who equates a recent burst of lightning with Daggoo's teeth; to various crew members characterizing Ahab's special crew in culturally insensitive terms; to the men who listen to Ishmael's recounting of the Town-Ho's story at the Golden Inn in Lima; to the gross and insensitive Capitalism that runs through the narrative in the hunting of the whales, Ishmael encounters ethnocentric behavior.

And, from his defensive start with Queequeg, Ishmael manages to rise above and grow considerably in intercultural sensitivity. Early in their relationship, Ishmael denigrates Queequeg and feels superior to him most of the time, but in time he begins to see ways in which Queequeg is superior. Even before these feelings, Ishmael minimizes Queequeg, showing that Ishmael's process closely follows Bennett's DMIS. Before long, Ishmael is using Queequeg's harpoon as a razor and accepting the harpooner's smoking in bed. In addition to sleeping together in the same bed, clear integration occurs in the highly symbolic Monkey-rope scene, linking the two as if by the life force of an umbilical cord. They are that attached, integrated. So that, in the end, Ishmael is, indeed, liminal. One of the first signs that Ishmael was moving toward liminality was in chapter 61, "Biographical." Ishmael's combination of accepting Queequeg while at the same time being defensive about him points to two sides at work in Ishmael, working simultaneously, indicative of the old Nathaniel Hawthorne–like balance or duality characteristic of one on the road to liminality.

One—The Nineteenth Century Romantic Novel

In his essay on "Trainer Competencies" in *Education for the Intercultural Experience*, Paige characterizes a good trainer with qualities such as openness, flexibility, tolerance of ambiguity, and sense of humor, to name a few (190–191). These are characteristics that Ishmael has. In another important essay from the same anthology the previous essay came from, Paige describes similar characteristics in the old context of constructive marginality, but he calls the state an empowered one (16). As this potential trainer, as the liminal one, Ishmael is the only survivor of the *Pequod*. In the introductory essay to his book, Cushner presents intercultural sensitivity theory that explains how Ishmael survives, for he states that those who have "a strong preference for interactions with similar others and an active avoidance of intercultural interactions will not fare well in 'a world' in which intercultural interactions are increasingly commonplace" (5). This is not to say that others aboard the *Pequod* are not culturally sensitive, for there are, namely Queequeg; however, Ishmael is different in several ways, especially in his ability to adapt and integrate with a plurality of views from the motley crew of the *Pequod*, and he is a writer, his book, this book, *Moby-Dick,* perhaps the best example of his liminality.

Intercultural sensitivity theory also connects with formal analyses of *Moby-Dick* in viewing Melville's theme of ambiguity. Ishmael realizes and accepts ambiguity. Wurzel writes, "Multiculturalism is the opposite of dogmatism, for it teaches us to accept the inevitable contradictions embedded in everything we learn" (5). Here comes that dreaded certainty again, death knell to sensitivity. Consider Ahab's monomania in opposition to Ishmael's intercultural sensitivity. Ishmael is able to take in multiple points of view, and from the variety create his own reality. This is almost exactly how Bennett explained the old constructive marginalism. In "Towards Ethnorelativism," Milton Bennett, the designer of the DMIS, defines a constructive marginal as one who is constantly creating his own reality (64), and Janet Bennett adds, the "constructive marginal is a person who is able to construct context intentionally and consciously for the purpose of creating his or her own identity" (113). These views seem hardly in conflict with liminality.

1. Melville's Liminal One

Ishmael might be a natural, though, at adapting multiple world-views, which is why reading, discussing, and writing about Melville's *Moby-Dick* would be helpful activities for those about to go abroad, and for those who cannot travel to experience different cultures, the novel, and Ishmael's characterization particularly, would, at least, expose them to the necessity of intercultural sensitivity. Ashwill writes, "there are ways of developing intercultural competence that do not necessarily include language learning and education abroad" (21). Definitely, studying Melville's masterpiece can be one of those ways. Ishmael would most likely appeal to Ashwill as a trainer, for he emphasizes that good education in intercultural sensitivity ought to stress the importance of interpersonal and relational skills and ambiguity tolerance and adaptivity, going as far as adding that such traits may very well characterize a modern leader.

2

The Scarlet Letter
Four Characters Under the DMIS

The Scarlet Letter reveals Hawthorne's literary spin on sensitivity psychologically within characters and toward others. Hawthorne filled *The Scarlet Letter*, published in 1850, with relational conflict. The general population of the setting—old Boston, with a scaffold rather than a well in the center of town to symbolize the town's ethics—denigrates and denies Hester Prynne, she with the bastard child, Pearl. The only character who has some level of acceptance of Hester, in true dramatic irony fashion, is the town's preacher, Arthur Dimmesdale, who also happens to be the father of Pearl. He, however, refuses to accept his fatherhood, hiding this side of himself, which Hawthorne symbolizes by having the preacher frequently cover his heart with his hands. The child, Pearl, is aptly named, for she is indeed precious under the lens of Bennett's DMIS because she accepts difference. Pearl would be representative of the transcendentalist uncorrupted by society, for she and her mother are forced to live on the outskirts of town, near the forest; moreover, growing up closer to nature than to the community of Boston, she accepts nature's gifts. Hawthorne takes the characterization of Pearl to the other side of Bennett's model, too. Similar to Emerson and Thoreau,

Pearl isn't very civil around society. She's very relational in nature, but she denigrates and denies in society. In "Becoming Interculturally Competent," Bennett tells us to mark growth in sensitivity to difference by looking for changes in knowledge, attitudes, or skills (75). The same marks, such as Pearl's, exist in Hawthorne's great novel.

Whereas Melville's novel provided opportunity to illustrate a character experiencing difference on a multicultural level aboard the *Pequod* and elsewhere, *The Scarlet Letter* is different. Bennett would describe the conflicts within the plot of the novel as monocultural. The communication takes place within a culture in which social difference is discouraged (*Basic Concepts* 5). That is the Puritan culture of Boston in the 1600s, the temporal setting of the novel. Typically, one thinks of intercultural sensitivity involving different cultures, but Bennett reminds us "there are other boundary conditions" (8). The big conflict at the start of the novel is that Hester Prynne has a child out of wedlock. Measuring sensitivity to difference within a community, using the DMIS, will reveal a community that does not accept difference. The good citizens of Boston do not accept Hester. They denigrate Hester by forcing her to stand on the scaffold at the center of town while holding her infant Pearl. They mark her by forcing her to wear a scarlet letter on the bosom of her dress. But what does the letter mean? Is it adulterer? Hawthorne loved his irony, and he characterized Hester as truly the best moral character in his narrative. Maybe the A means angel? Others have suggested Ambiguity since the concept seems to be at the heart of one of Hawthorne's major Romantic themes. Bennett actually lists intolerance of ambiguity when listing other kinds of differences one could study (81). The Puritans of America may be one of the most intolerant broods on this continent, these pilgrims who executed individuals for really no good reason during the Salem witch trials. After Hester's ignominy on the scaffold, she is returned to jail, and we get our first relationship when she receives a visitor from the past.

The arrival of Roger Chillingworth in the plot allows us to move our focus on sensitivity to difference—from the general crowd around the scaffold for Hester's punishment, which some, in true denigrating fashion, thought wasn't enough—to a one-on-one relationship to analyze under the lens of the DMIS. When we first meet Chillingworth, Hawthorne characterizes him in bi-cultural ways. He is standing next to a Native American and is dressed in "civilized and savage costume" (52). At the least, such dress denotes some adaptation on Bennett's scale. He stands in the crowd witnessing Hester's public ignominy. He is Hester's husband, thought dead. She is experiencing public denigration, and he is a part of the crowd and does nothing to end her suffering. When the two recognize one another, he signals to her to keep quiet, denigrating her and their relationship, showing no sign of being the knight in shining armor, accepting her difference in his love for her, sweeping her off the scaffold in a swashbuckling manner and carrying her away where they live together forever. He can't do that because in a matter of moments Chillingworth has had the chilling idea that he can best have his revenge on the one who has put Hester in this place, one who seems to be unable to accept Hester as is, by remaining a stranger with no connection to Hester. Chillingworth, rather than accepting Hester as is, chooses a kind of denial of Hester, by ignoring her, using her only as a tool to fulfill his budding ideas of revenge. The denial does not last.

Chillingworth goes to Hester later, but only to feed the revenge, moving to denigrating feelings toward her that are shared by the rest of the community; however, Chillingworth has different reasons that he hides. On the surface, his denigration exists within the context of viewing Hester as different, as having a different worldview. After her time on the scaffold, Hester is returned to prison, and Chillingworth visits her there as a doctor. As the narrator told us of his dress before, Master Brackett, the jailer, describes him in bicultural terms, "a man of skill in all Christian modes of physical science, and likewise familiar with whatever the savage people could teach, in respect to medicinal herbs and roots that grew in the forest" (61). Master Brackett continues the community predilection toward denigration. However, this second detail of Chillingworth's character reveals a man practiced in adapting from different cultures. Chillingworth's examples of adaption were not, though, the result of an intention. He sailed to the New World ahead of Hester, was shipwrecked, and captured by some indigenous peoples. Hester, following, found herself alone in Boston. Now, he visits her, assuring her, declaring "I seek no vengeance, plot no evil against thee" (65). It's the father Chillingworth wants, but Hester will not tell. Hester has adapted the secret, showing a strong relational bond with the father. Chillingworth essentially goes beyond denigration to denial with Hester, only seeing her as a way to seek his revenge, referring to their relationship as a thing to be scored and assuring her that they are balanced, even. Chillingworth leaves confident that he will be able to read the sin in the heart of the father, who, once found, will suffer Chillingworth's capacity for denial on another level, torturing a man, slowly killing him. Such behavior posits Roger Chillingworth as a villain. On Bennett's scale, he's at the very bottom of ethnocentric relating based on the recognition of and interview with Hester in chapters three and four.

Roger Chillingworth next appears four chapters later (and two to three years later) during Hester's meeting with Governor Bellingham in his hall on the topic of Pearl's fate. Chillingworth is there but only because Arthur Dimmesdale is there. Dimmesdale appears briefly in the third chapter. He is under some enormous dramatic irony as he is exhorted by others to try to convince Hester to repent and confess. Governor Bellingham urges Dimmesdale with "the responsibility of this woman's soul lies greatly with you" (57). Hawthorne describes the preacher as off course with the rest of society, a bit lost. He doesn't relate well with people but is able to work with that by coming across as childlike when relating due to his so innocent soul. The act seems to work for the preacher, for as a preacher his social difference is accepted; however, there's the side of him that same society would view more darkly. Russell Reising writes, "Dimmesdale is prevented from confessing his sin as much by the community's view of him as by his own view" (70). Reising and others posit denial within Dimmesdale, denying a part of himself, and this is where *The Scarlet Letter* can be viewed as having a psychological component with Bennett's DMIS. Since that time on the scaffold in which he accuses Hester of denying the father the opportunity to repent and confess by refusing to name him, Dimmesdale has been accompanied by Roger Chillingworth.

2. *The Scarlet Letter*

Dimmesdale has been physically suffering since that time on the scaffold, and Chillingworth is serving as the preacher's doctor. Hawthorne describes them as close. The community thinks Dimmesdale has been working too hard. But, clearly, as Dimmesdale's doctor, Chillingworth is failing, yet Dimmesdale has not dismissed him. Geoff Bender suggests, "Dimmesdale masochistically submits to Chillingworth's sadistic advances in mutually pleasurable encounters that, while not necessarily genitally engaged, are yet as sexual as the moment of Pearl's conception" (59). At the least, Dimmesdale accepts this unknown man, said to be a doctor, and they integrate. They live together. Chillingworth's acceptance in this relationship, though, is, again, based on revenge. His is an act, and many have argued that the good doctor is slowly poisoning Dimmesdale, pretending to attend to him as a physician. So, both men deny, Chillingworth in his vengeance, and Dimmesdale in his silence; furthermore, both suffer. Hester notices it as the interview at Governor Bellingham's seems to be winding down and not in Hester's favor. To her, Chillingworth is now uglier, and "his dark complexion seemed to have grown duskier, and his figure more misshapen" (96). Previously, Hawthorne had described Chillingworth as a kind of hunchback, but his condition appears to be worsening just as Dimmesdale's does while both are experiencing issues in relating.

But, really, only Dimmesdale's denial works within the context of Bennett's DMIS. In fact, Dimmesdale appears to be in the stage of reversal. Rather than seeing himself as natural, which he is, and the intolerant Puritan community as insensitive to difference, Dimmesdale sees himself as they would see him if they knew the truth. He cannot accept the part of him that marks him different than the rest of the community. Similar to the traveler abroad who accepts the different culture and denigrates his native culture, in this monocultural tale, Dimmesdale accepts what would be the Puritan community position on the preacher if they knew the truth as he does. This denial on the part of Dimmesdale is at once in both a psychological and social context. He must deny a part of himself in order to keep his job. If we consider Dimmesdale's action at the bottom stage of denial within Bennett's scale, then we can see how relating is linked to what seems to be one of the major themes of the novel, what Richard Chase describes as the "moral and psychological results of sin" (72). It would seem Dimmesdale's denial functions on a psychological level within himself, denying a part of his humanity, and in masquerading as a pure, innocent preacher it has its social level, too. Reising, too, notes "the novel's social world" (70). Dimmesdale must act the way society expects him to. He would not be in compliance with the rules of his community if he were true; therefore, in his everyday relating with others he also denies them the true Dimmesdale. He consents, agreeing with society that what he has done is morally outrageous and subsequently must be hidden from society if one were to remain in it.

He is not true to himself or society. This can be readily seen during the big scene of Hester's interview in the hall of Governor Bellingham, who is about to rule that Pearl be taken from Hester to be properly raised. This threat, a denial of Hester's motherhood because she is raising Pearl in a fashion different than the Puritan community would prefer, is action at the bottom of Bennett's scale. This forces Hester to threaten to slough off the adaptation in which she accepted Dimmesdale's need for the truth to be secret. She is now willing to deny Dimmesdale's need for secrecy to keep her child, forcing Dimmesdale to persuade Governor Bellingham to allow Hester to keep Pearl. Dimmesdale argues passionately on Hester's behalf to keep the child, referring to the child as her salvation, something the child cannot give Dimmesdale because he cannot accept her and keep his job. Dimmesdale says, "Herein is the sinful mother happier than the sinful father" (98). Dimmesdale's earnestness does not go unnoticed by Chillingworth.

Chillingworth's denial exists primarily on the social level, in his deception of the community for his purpose of remaining with Dimmesdale, but more importantly in his relationship with Dimmesdale, who is unaware of Chillingworth's dark purpose that he made clear during his interview with Hester in prison. It would seem that these two to three years that have passed in the narrative has been a time in which Roger Chillingworth is pretty sure Dimmesdale is the father but not completely sure, and it would further seem that once Chillingworth is sure of the target for his revenge, he would slide down Bennett's DMIS into the lowest levels of ethnocentric behavior and see Dimmesdale as different. Yet, he must be sure.

After the episode at Governor Bellingham's, Hawthorne takes the reader deeper into the relationship between Dimmesdale and Chillingworth. Bennett's DMIS will help gauge the behavior of these two characters objectively, avoiding a more moral plain. As Frederick Crews writes, "*The Scarlet Letter* has more to do with perverse emotional strategies than with moral evil" (xii). Hawthorne writes that Chillingworth had chosen Dimmesdale as his spiritual guide early upon his arrival, and, that, due in part to this decision, the townspeople accepted Chillingworth as exemplary "at least as regarded the outward forms of a religious life" (102). But, inside Chillingworth seethes with vengeance. Dimmesdale cannot accept his own sin, but Chillingworth accepts his own motive of revenge. His denying the Puritan community from knowing this is what makes his relating more social than psychological. The Puritan community's misreading of Chillingworth's strong interests in Dimmesdale is another one of Hawthorne's fine examples of dramatic irony, a literary element that courses through the conversation between Chillingworth and Dimmesdale in chapters 9 and 10.

The conversation reveals the conflict Dimmesdale experiences. Bennett, in *Basic Concepts*, writes of conflicts being created by predominant experiences (130). Dimmesdale's adultery has brought him to the point that he wishes he were dead. His reversal has taken him that deep into denying himself, seeing himself so different from the community that adores him. Bennett also tells us to lookout for nonverbal communication (63–64), and during this scene, Dimmesdale again puts his hand over his heart, a symbolic gesture to hide his sin, to deny the community the truth. Hawthorne shows Dimmesdale on these pages attracted to revealing his true self, a conflict Richard Chase describes as the "thwarting of the emotional life" (72), but the force of society is too strong. Again, on a monocultural level, Dimmesdale accepts the Puritan society but denies the part of himself that he views as different from that Puritan cultural norm, which is why Hawthorne writes that he stayed "within the limits of what [the] church defined as orthodox" (105). Hawthorne adds that Chillingworth is with Dimmesdale almost all the time now and that the community is changing its view of Chillingworth, some thinking that the physical deterioration that has accompanied Dimmesdale's suffering character may be linked to Chillingworth's presence; however, nobody intervenes. Elie Wiesel states in his 1999 speech, "The Perils of Indifference," "for the person who is indifferent, his or her neighbor are of no consequence. And, therefore, their lives are meaningless" (para. 5). In Bennett's DMIS, indifference is denial, the lowest level of ethnocentrism.

Chapter 10 ends with a climax for Chillingworth. Having suspected Dimmesdale as the father of Pearl, at the end of this chapter Chillingworth is certain. Change is integral to almost any climax in literature, and Bennett affirms the simple essence of change in *Basic Concepts* as a strong indicator of an individual progressing through the process of intracultural sensitivity (49). In this monocultural setting, Chillingworth now becomes the ur representative of the Puritan community and their tolerance for difference. If you think the women watching Hester suffer on the scaffold were insensitive, Chillingworth is about to take it to another level. The thing with Chillingworth is that he is now going to descend further down the relational scale of Bennett's DMIS. Hawthorne opens the next chapter with "after the incident last described, the intercourse between the clergyman and the physician, though externally the same, was really of another character than it had previously been" (119). But how did Chillingworth change so?

Chapter 10 of *The Scarlet Letter* builds to this climactic, life-changing predominant experience for Roger Chillingworth. The chapter opens describing how Chillingworth has been overcome with vengeance, creating in him the kind of monomania seen in Ahab in Melville's *Moby-Dick*. He senses that Dimmesdale has a dark secret. Soon, Hawthorne takes us into a hypothetical conversation with Chillingworth feeding Dimmesdale opportunity to accept himself and overcome the psychological denial. When Dimmesdale asks herbalist Chillingworth about a weed, Chillingworth states he found it growing from a grave, suggesting the roots trace down to a heart buried with "some hideous secret" (112). Chillingworth may be viewed here more relationally using Bennett's scale, for he has spent enough time around Dimmesdale, much like a traveler in a foreign land, to enable him to accept that Dimmesdale is hiding something. He has the experience. Chillingworth thinking Dimmesdale should let out the truth would certainly fulfill his revenge, forcing the fall of Dimmesdale's pastoral career; however, it is, ironically, a relational triumph if we consider that Dimmesdale has moved beyond his reversal and is accepting that part of himself that marks him as different. Again, Bennett marks what needs to occur as one moves into acceptance, and one of those things is the individual needs to reconcile unity and diversity (*Basic Concepts* 100). Dimmesdale needs to square his dark side, which makes him different, at least in his mind, with the rest of himself, which seems to be in unity with the Puritan community. Hester is already there when it comes to squaring oneself with one's dark side, but Dimmesdale continues his denial throughout the hypothetical conversation. Chillingworth argues the revelation would inspire repentance among the flock while Dimmesdale believes he must mask his dark side in order to best help his parishioners. Dimmesdale cannot take the hypothetical conversation any more as it gets too close, and he rushes out. That night, Chillingworth snuck to a sleeping Dimmesdale and moved aside the vestment covering the preacher's bosom. It is a "eureka" moment for Chillingworth as there is seemingly some ambiguous sign on Dimmesdale's chest, and Chillingworth is now hell bent in his monomania.

Though Chillingworth may now have a one-track mind, *The Scarlet Letter* is latent in multiplicity when it comes to ambiguous signs. The multiplicity of meaning associated with Hawthorne's ambiguous symbolism connects to Bennett's DMIS. The symbols force readers to think in different ways. Some of Hawthorne's characters in the novel would benefit from following that lead. Chillingworth and Dimmesdale have only one way of looking at one very important thing in each man's life. Dimmesdale can only see his sin as something that makes him too different to be accepted by the community. Chillingworth can only see Dimmesdale as the object of his vengeance. Chillingworth has next to no interest in changing his course, but Dimmesdale longs for acceptance. He attempts half-hearted confessions of how vile he is, never linking himself with Hester and Pearl. Still, these acts demonstrate a move toward ethnorelational behavior because Dimmesdale views himself as having a different worldview than the good people of the community. His desire to be accepted by them is akin to a traveler wishing to be accepted abroad. The ironies are the community is just as flawed, if not more so, that his efforts to appear vile only make him more revered by the community, and that this guy living with Dimmesdale to be of aid may very well be a driving force toward killing him.

Dimmesdale longs to be accepted by this intolerant brood, to appear on the scaffold as Hester and Pearl did and still be accepted. Such an act would, at least, point to Dimmesdale maybe psychologically accepting that different part of himself. The preacher even goes to the scaffold, but only at night. Then, one night he sees Hester and Pearl there and invites them to stand on the scaffold with him. Still, it is late at night. Nobody would see them. Roger Chillingworth, though, walks by and sees them. It is a story. He had been attending to a dying patient and returning home saw all three upon the scaffold. Despite Dimmesdale's desperate pleas, fueled by a fear of Chillingworth, for Hester to reveal the truth, Hester "remembered her oath, and was silent" (134). This is a big relational conflict for Hester, and, furthermore, she will not reveal to Dimmesdale her relationship with Chillingworth. She keeps secrets for both men, secrets that if out would mark both men as different and subject to the kind of ethnocentric behavior from the community that Hester is experiencing. That's very empathic of Hester. The next morning, Dimmesdale continues to deny the difference within himself when he lies to a sexton about leaving his glove on the scaffold, something Dimmesdale must deny knowing anything about, for he cannot be considered as someone who has been out on the scaffold in the middle of the night and keep his job. The section also brings up a meteor seen by many that night. Dimmesdale had seen this same meteor, and, in fact, thought of it as the letter A when he saw it, but when the sexton reveals the community perception that the sight in the night sky was indeed an A and signified Angel to represent the passing of Chillingworth's patient, Dimmesdale denies knowing anything about it. Being out would mark him as different.

Hester has accepted the actions that have marked her as different from the rest of the Puritan community. Hawthorne's narrative reveals interesting insights into sensitivity to difference when the focus is on Hester and her scarlet letter. In *Basic Concepts*, Bennett writes about how different cultural values can be seen through the lens of the basic nature of human beings (79). Hawthorne seems to explore this through his ambiguous symbolism with the letter A, Hester's own letter A, which she is bound to wear on her bosom to mark her as an Adulteress. After the night of the meteor, the next chapter in *The Scarlet Letter* shows how many in the Puritan community have changed their view of Hester, represented when Hawthorne writes, "Such helpfulness was found in her—so much power to do, power to sympathize—that many people refused to interpret the scarlet A by its original signification. They said that it meant Able; so strong was Hester Prynne, with a woman's strength" (138). Many scholars have written on how there are two worldviews in Hawthorne's novel. One is associated with religion and the Old World, and Dimmesdale would fall into that grouping, while another view is more secular and linked to the New World, and Hester fits there. It is an accepting world within Bennett's DMIS.

Hawthorne clearly characterizes Hester as one who is sensitive to difference. Nina Baym writes, "Re-entering civil life, adorned with the letter by her own choice, Hester moves Puritan Boston from the Dark Ages toward enlightened modernity" (44). To the sick and poor, Hester gives comfort, clothing, and food. Hawthorne uses parallelism to emphasize Hester stands out from the others in town for her sensitivity to difference, writing "none so ready as she," and "none so self-devoted as Hester" (137). The scarlet letter was meant to punish Hester, to mark her as different and ostracize her from the community. She does live on the outskirts of town, but she acts so selflessly and accepts those in a community who do not accept her. In time, the community, though, cannot deny Hester's good, relational acts, and she becomes more accepted. Like her A, Hester takes on different worldviews. Living on the edge of town close to the forest, one could characterize Hester as a constructive marginal; however, she integrates so well that Bennett's newer leaning toward liminality may better suit Hester. Reising seems to recognize this liminality when he writes, "As the 'A' gradually accrues greater ranges of meaning and represents a variety of positive senses, so does our understanding of Hester" (72). Toward a community that denigrates and denies her, Hester accepts the community nonetheless, adapts over years, and integrates into society still wearing the A, still marked as different so that Hester's story in Hawthorne's novel becomes a wonderful example of relational living as both sides change.

This change has a feminist context that fits into sensitivity to difference. As man oppresses woman, so the community oppresses Hester. The function of the scarlet letter is to mark her as different, as one to be shunned. The scarlet letter was supposed to make Hester like the others in the community. This is why Hawthorne, in a single sentence paragraph so that it stands out, writes, "The scarlet letter had not done its office" (142). It is also why Sacvan Bercovitch latched onto the phrase because he recognizes the lack of acceptance in the Puritan community and their efforts to promote their single worldview within their community. He writes, "*The Scarlet Letter* is a story of socialization in which the point of socialization is not to conform, but to consent" (xiii). Hester foils their plans. She embraces the dark side that the scarlet letter represents. This dark side, manifested in her adultery, is what marks her as different. It is what the Puritan community cannot accept. Most agree that Hester, in embracing the community that denigrates and denies her, rises above that community as a relational human, her character easily seen within the ethnorelative half of Bennett's DMIS, and all thanks, ironically, to the thing, the scarlet letter, that was meant to subjugate Hester. Richard Chase writes, "Hawthorne certainly believed that no adulthood, no society, no tragic sense of life could exist without the knowledge of evil," and a page later he writes that the novel "has a feminist theme" (72–73). To be sure, Hester is oppressed because of her difference, her adultery, but serves as a mid-nineteenth-century female model in a novel that does not come out until around two years after the inaugural women's rights convention held in Seneca Falls, New York, in 1848.

Pearl also scores in the ethnorelative stages of Bennett's DMIS. Shortly after the scene in which Hester stands up to Roger Chillingworth, telling him that she will tell the truth to Dimmesdale, Pearl earns more of Hawthorne's attention in the novel. One of the first anecdotes Hawthorne gives us is of Pearl pelting sea birds with rocks. She hits one, she thinks, in typical Hawthorne ambiguity, breaking its wing. She then changes, sympathizing with the bird that is "as wild as Pearl herself" (152). Pearl's wildness is characterized as natural. She has been raised outside of society. How she relates to anyone or anything is not a rationally conscious behavior. Chase writes, "Pearl represents the intuitive," and he associates her with the unconscious (78–79). Like many Romantics, such as Thoreau in his 1848 *On the Duty of Civil Disobedience,* Hawthorne seems to be promoting the relational powers of the unconscious when it comes to sensitivity to difference.

A little later, Hester and Pearl meet Dimmesdale in the forest. Pearl will not accept him. Dimmesdale reports that no children seem to accept him. Pearl, in fact, who has been playing by a brook side while Dimmesdale and Hester talked, will not even accept her mother anymore. Dimmesdale and Hester had been talking about idealistic plans to escape the intolerant community, and in doing so, Hester removed her letter and let her hair down. Pearl does not appear to even recognize her mother. When Hester resumes wearing the scarlet letter and reties her hair, Pearl accepts her. She still cannot accept Dimmesdale, though, seeing him as one who does not accept her since he will not, in Pearl's words, "go back with us, hand in hand, we three together, into the town" (182). Pearl has no problem accepting Native Americans and swarthy mariners at the holiday procession near the end of the novel, and before she came up to Dimmesdale and Hester in the forest, Hawthorne tells us that she made friends with animals such as squirrels and foxes and that a wolf even came up to her "and offered his savage head to be petted by her hand" (176). Simon O. Lesser writes of this forest scene that it "shows the virtue and perhaps the beauty of impulses we either deny or gratify" (188). Bennett's DMIS would have Dimmesdale denying his impulses while the natural Pearl accepts all except what she deems as unaccepting of her or, worse, is evil in her eyes.

Two

The Nineteenth-Century Realistic Novel

The Country of the Pointed Firs and *The American*

3

Relating to the World in Down East, Maine

Sensitivity in Jewett's *Country*

I wrote my dissertation on Sarah Orne Jewett's 1896 master-piece, *The Country of the Pointed Firs*. When I first wrote the dissertation, which was later published by Mellen as *Sarah Orne Jewett's Feminine Pastoral Vision,* I was unaware of Milton J. Bennett and how his theory applies to Jewett's novel even though I was aware that *Country* was published in an era of growing tourism. Now, in light of Bennett's Developmental Model of Intercultural Sensitivity (DMIS) (again, still highly respected in the study-abroad field now for over twenty years), the relationships Jewett created serve as models of intercultural sensitivity. The results from closely analyzing the relationships within the framework of Bennett's theory allows for literature, again, to prepare students for difference, whether they study abroad or stay in their own backyards, and specifically for this novel, while Jewett's alternating structure from episodes of isolation to episodes of relation lends itself to feminine and pastoral gazes, it is through the lens of intercultural sensitivity theory in which the novel presents a model of the process from ethnocentrism toward ethnorelativism.

To be sure, Milton J. Bennett's model lends itself well to analyzing how characters in narratives relate to one another and how the relationships grow, or not. I have tried to show, under the lens of Bennett's model, how two classic American novels have addressed intercultural sensitivity. Ishmael's growing relationship with Queequeg in Herman Melville's *Moby-Dick* mirrors Bennett's model and is instructive when considering dealing with difference when the worldview is from another world, and Nathaniel Hawthorne's *The Scarlet Letter* presents the conflict of confronting a different worldview within the same small community. The purpose here is to present how several relationships in Jewett's *Country* serve as positive models, the episodes focusing on relation, illustrating the process of relational growth that frames Bennett's DMIS, a growth the nameless narrator of the novel takes from ethnocentrism to ethnorelativism.

To review some of the basic characteristics of Bennett's DMIS, within each half, there are three phases. Beginning with ethnocentrism, the phases pass from denial, to defense, and then minimization. Lending to the utility of Bennett's model, the phases are almost self-evident. The phase of denial characterizes one who doesn't even recognize another who is different. In the next phase, defense, the same character, forced to accept the existence of those who are different, will nonetheless denigrate them. And, in the final phase of ethnocentrism, the same character grows to liking something about this other even though the trait is something that the character feels he shares with this other person of difference. Bennett's ethnorelative stages also clearly evince the relational process. After minimization, and first trait within the ethnorelative stage is acceptance, and after a character accepts difference in another, the next phase passes into adaptation, the act of embracing some characteristic from a different culture. Finally, a character would demonstrate ultimate relational growth within Bennett's model by integrating with those who are different (21–71). Again, Janet Bennett takes the process to a conclusion when she writes of the older constructive marginal view, writing the following line that bears repeating. "While various cultural groups may seek his allegiance, he appears to claim for himself an identity that is beyond any singular cultural perspective" (110). But, here with Jewett's nameless narrator, the integration is bicultural on two levels involving feminist and pastoral gazes. Milton Bennett accounts for different worldviews affecting sensitivity to difference in *Basic Concepts*, writing "there are other boundary conditions" (8). Jewett's nameless narrator, though, does not seem marginalized in the older sense of the constructive marginal. She seems more liminal, and the symbolism of connection is quite strong at novels end. More so than Ishmael, she seems fit for Milton Bennett's new view involving liminality, the expansion of worldviews without the negative marginalization.

Jewett's point of view through the nameless narrator visiting the country from Boston and the alternating, pastoral structure of the plot lend themselves to dealing with difference; in fact, much great scholarly work has been done evincing how relational a novel it is even though the novel also shows a more exclusionary vision. Perhaps we shouldn't be too surprised. As Robert Shulman writes while analyzing a contemporary of Jewett's, Stephen Crane, late nineteenth-century American society has the "tendency to isolate individuals, to fragment selves and relations, and to substitute technological, contractual, and bureaucratic ties for those of human compassion" (441–442). The more exclusionary view of *Country* also has its scholarly output. Significant is early work by Elizabeth Ammons, Susan Gillman, and Sandra Zagarell, each of whom has an essay on this subject in June Howard's essential 1994 anthology, *New Essays on The Country of the Pointed Firs*. Gillman, for instance, writes about how the good people of Dunnet Landing visited by our Boston narrator view a foreign presence as threatening (106). More recently, Holly Jackson and Thomas Strychacz have addressed this issue. Though Jackson seems to see more that's relational in *Country* than ethnocentric, she still spends the first part of her important essay on the subject of "race suicide" (264–268), and she reinforces Shulman's view on American society when she writes of relationships maintained within decay leading to clannishness. Strychacz also sees a dividing factor, writing of Dunnet Landing, Jewett's spatial setting for the novel, as a nativist state (55). And we are all familiar with Jewett's *The Story of the Normans,* her non-fiction celebration of the dominant culture that populates the fictional world of *Country.*

However, more scholars prefer, at least emotionally, to read *Country* for its relational side. *Country* works well with intercultural sensitivity theory and in particular Bennett's DMIS. Of the genres Jewett's masterpiece falls into, the pastoral novel with a feminine point of view and theme works well with Bennett since Jewett's feminine pastoral vision focuses on relating. The spatial setting of Dunnet Landing is a pastoral matriarchy into which Jewett puts her narrator, an outsider, a woman from Boston in quest of solitude to write, characterizing her in a more competitive, male-oriented urban way. The narrator of *Country* experiences alternating episodes, one with another character valuing the city and the masculine followed by another chapter with a different character valuing the country and the feminine, similar to the singing matches upon which the pastoral tradition is founded in the likes of Theocritus. At the climactic Bowden Reunion, the narrator eats a pie with Bowden written on it, symbolizing her communion with the country, which, because of the feminine point of view allows the city v. country conflict to take air as male v. female. In *The Rites of Passage,* Arnold Van Gennep emphasizes that a shared meal is essentially an incorporation ritual (20). The narrator, in the end, has become more relational by expanding to four worldviews: city, country, male, and female. This is the basis for a multiculturality that is unlike assimilation or melting pot thinking that creates a sense of controlling outside forces. This is openness. Jewett's narrative has taken the nameless narrator from seeking seclusion to being able to relate to the isolated Elijah Tilley. The novel and Bennett's model follow a similar path. Yes, Jewett's feminine pastoral vision compliments Bennett's DMIS, and the alternating structure to *Country* echoes the pastoral tradition of two shepherds having a singing match. One side of her structure presents relational living in a rural matriarchy while the other side presents isolatos, creating conflict for the narrator who originally came to Dunnet Landing for the seclusion to write but begins growing relational in a pattern mirroring Bennett's model.

3. Relating to the World in Down East, Maine

Indeed, important feminist scholarship covers the notion of *Country* promoting a more relational life. Josephine Donovan, Marcia McClintock-Folsom, Margaret Roman, and Laurie Shannon, among others, have done outstanding work on the subject. Even Ammons, who addresses the exclusionary side of the debate, recognizes that Jewett's novel is "not grounded in separation and aggression but in connection, in feelings of intimate relatedness to others" (83–84). The nameless narrator makes connections with almost everyone she meets in Dunnet Landing, exhibiting a wide range of inclusiveness and relational skill. Donovan characterizes the nameless narrator of the novel as an "alienated urban daughter seeking to reconnect with and preserve the matriarchal ... and escape from the masculine" (222). Make no mistake about the ways *Country* seems to want us to think when we read it with this hybrid gaze of the pastoral and feminine. Robin Magowan writes of the Joanna episode, which is clearly within the urban, male, ethnocentric side of this argument, that her tale is "a moral lesson of the dangers implicit in the wish for seclusion" (424).

Recent criticism viewing *Country* through this relational lens persists. In 2013, Debbie Lelekis analyzes the setting of the novel as women healing community. In another example of, appropriately, hybrid theory, Marcia Littenberg in one of the more contemporary anthologies on Jewett, *Jewett and Her Contemporaries: Reshaping the Canon*, addresses *Country* through ecofeminism, a discussion that also plays well with Bennett's DMIS. Notice the relational possibilities with the vegetable kingdom when Littenberg writes that ideas "of moral superiority and domination could be replaced by an ethic that emphasizes conservation, mutual respect, and acceptance of variety and difference" (141). In fact, the editor of that anthology, Karen Kilcup, also writes eloquently on the topic for the 2004 *American Writers: Classics*. In her Jewett chapter, she asserts that through "the portraits of Elijah (Tilley) and others, Jewett suggests the frail connections between and among people of different races, ethnicities, genders, and classes, and she invites readers to ponder the possibilities and difficulties of establishing such connections" (79). Maybe this analysis could serve as a model, for Milton Bennett writes in

Basic Concepts that "having more people in the world who are aware of perspective is a good thing" (39). When it comes to prizing empathy, Bennett and Jewett are on the same page.

The point of view in *Country* illustrates a sensitivity process through plot, conflict, and climax, and by setting her narrative within the framework of a summer visit, Jewett give readers the symbolic process of season to suggest a life cycle although, in this case, the cycle of life and death focuses on the death of a more ethnocentric self and the birth of a more relational self. Jewett writes in the final chapter, "So we die before our own eyes; so we see some chapters of our lives come to their natural end" (161). Just as Ishmael gains sensitivity toward Queequeg, in *Country,* Captain Littlepage in Jewett's *Country* gains sensitivity toward Gaffett while Jewett's nameless narrator gains sensitivity toward Littlepage, other isolatos in the novel, and ultimately just about the whole community of Dunnet Landing. So, to that end, it is time for a close analysis of Jewett's *Country* that will demonstrate how these relationships between characters can help foster a more sorely needed ethnorelative world.

Denial, the lowest phase of ethnocentrism in Bennett's DMIS, is harsh, and Jewett presents its existence in a couple ways. First, in chapter three, the nameless narrator reveals how she feels about her setting and its people. Jewett writes, "Selfish as it may appear, the retired situation seemed to possess great advantages" (36). The narrator has set up shop in a Dunnet Landing schoolhouse to write. Being away from others has the intent of helping her write. She has ostensibly denied the community in her "retired situation," adding that she "spent many days there quite undisturbed" (36). The selfishness of seclusion is a denial of others. She uses them like things. Although, characterizing her as an artist, Jewett has steered us right into Bennett's DMIS, for early in *Basic Concepts,* he links intercultural sensitivity with the artist (20). Other characters in the novel, though, reinforce denial. Littlepage, Joanna Todd, and Elijah Tilley all represent characters in denial of others. Tilley is alone, only existing within the illusionary company of his deceased wife. Joanna secludes herself on an island, and Littlepage, too, is disconnected from the community. These characters serve the nameless narrator as cautions of remaining in this lowest stage of ethnocentrism, and help propel her through the process of becoming more relational. Note some symbolic imagery used to characterize Littlepage. On the way to the Bowden Reunion, a relational event if there ever was one, the nameless narrator and her travelling companions, Mrs. Todd and her mother, Mrs. Blackett, pass Littlepage's home. The narrator tells us that he "was sitting behind his closed window as I passed by, watching for someone who never came" (118). The pastoral character of *Country* provides this imagery its symbolic heft of denial.

The key first step in Bennett's DMIS is to move from denial to defense, recognizing the existence of others but denigrating them, and Jewett's *Country* illuminates this phase as well. Veritably prophesying writers in the early part of the twentieth century, Jewett offers society at large as practicing defensive postures when it comes to meeting difference. Captain Littlepage, marooned once with a man named Gaffett, retells to the nameless narrator Gaffett's tale of a fantastic island with ghost-like figures in a seemingly other world. In telling, he tells of when he has previously told the tale, adding "those who have laughed at me little know how much reason my ideas are based on" (45). Specifically, the scientific community belittles Littlepage by disdaining his story. Some scientists don't respond to his letters. Perhaps denial coming from these highly specialized scientists should not be too surprising, but Mrs. Todd also puts down Littlepage. Once, while talking about Native Americans leaving a captive isolated on an island, she subtly alluded to Littlepage and Gaffett's tale about the discovery of a ghost island, but the nameless narrator adds that Mrs. Todd said this grimly, showing Mrs. Todd dismissive of both stories. Short of calling Littlepage crazy, she suggests he is difficult to relate to, primarily due to his obsession with Gaffett's tale, and this rubs off on the nameless narrator when she first meets Littlepage and he begins telling his tale. Early on in his fantastic talk she remembers what Mrs. Todd had said about him, how he had "overset his mind" (44), and she initially does not believe Littlepage's great tale about a great discovery, scoring low in Bennett's sensitivity to difference within the DMIS.

The incidents of defensive posturing in *Country* are there. The nameless narrator had been defensive before even arriving. However, once there, and having come to Dunnet Landing to seek seclusion, she is defensive about the lack of it in Mrs. Todd's house, disparaging the very relational character she will ultimately embrace. It's a bumpy ride toward ethnorelativism. Midway through the novel, the narrator, having made significant progress toward becoming more relational, slides backwards with the pending arrival of a guest to Mrs. Todd's house. Mrs. Fosdick's visit is described in words such as *strange, invasion, objection,* and *apprehension.* And, it turns out, Mrs. Fosdick herself takes defensive positions when met with difference. At one point during her stay, she complains of the sameness she finds in people. Yet another example of defensive posturing in *Country* comes from Parson Dimmick, he of the allegorical name, like Littlepage. Dimmick acts defensively when visiting Joanna Todd, a woman who feels her sin makes her unfit to be around others and so isolates herself on Shell-heap Island, the same place where the captive of the Native Americans was supposed to have been. Dimmick deflates Joanna's spirituality, her faith, missing the Bible on the shelf and accusing her of not practicing her faith very well. Furthermore, note how Mrs. Todd behaves defensively about her true love and his family, pointing out to the narrator that it was class difference that kept them apart all those years ago, an attitude that hasn't changed much over the years since we see Mrs. Todd continuing to reproach her true love's family at the Bowden Reunion. When a certain member of that family passes Mrs. Todd's sight, she angrily says, "I expected she'd come pleasantin' around just to show off an' say afterwards she was acquainted" (136). The Blacketts might be angels, living on Green Island, but most of the other central characters of *Country* have defense issues.

Jewett also takes us from defense to minimization in *Country.* This third stage in Bennett's DMIS, the stage in which ethnocentrism occurs through accepting only similar traits in people of difference and the last within the ethnocentric half of the whole process, rears its ugly head in a few ways. Captain Littlepage, for instance, can be characterized as his own worst enemy when it comes to being relational as he seems to only admire those, like himself, who have seen the world. Similarly, Parson Dimmick appears to only appreciate the spirituality in his flock, failing to accept the common character of the sea town, which can be readily observed when Mrs. Todd relates his inability to stay seated in rough waters. Though his presence in Jewett's *Country* is brief, Joanna's would-be husband also demonstrates minimalizing behavior when Mrs. Todd characterizes him as someone who is only interested in something about another when it is to his economic advantage.

Perhaps one of the scariest specimens of minimization happens at the Bowden Reunion. Here, that exclusionary vision becomes clear near the end of the reunion when the nameless narrator muses that the coterie she has witnessed "is an instinct of the heart—it is more than a birthright, or a custom; and lesser rights were forgotten in the claim to a common inheritance" (141). In the seaside town of Dunnet Landing, blood is still thicker than water. However, at least minimization is some acceptance. It is a starting point, and when there appears to be no common ground, then one must be found. Take for example the initial relationship between Mrs. Fosdick and the nameless narrator. Seemingly fated for a difficult time relating to one another, Mrs. Todd starts the two toward a better relationship. Knowing that Mrs. Fosdick will want to hear about her and the nameless narrator's earlier visit to Green Island to see Mrs. Todd's mother and brother, Mrs. Todd suggests the nameless narrator relate their visit while she goes into the kitchen. This final stage in the ethnocentrism half of Bennett's DMIS is a transitional stage. From here, if they progress, characters move to acceptance of difference in others.

The acceptance of difference in others, the first stage in the relational side of Bennett's model, courses though *Country*. It can be minimal at first as when Mrs. Todd tells of the level of acceptance the community seems to have for Mari Harris, the woman who attends to Captain Littlepage, though not very well in the eyes of Dunnet Landing; still, "they treated her with anxious civility when they met her face to face" (40). It can also waver, especially if the character going through the process of becoming more relational is early in the process as with the narrator whose lukewarm acceptance of Captain

Littlepage and his wild tale comes and goes. In referencing Bennett's DMIS, the 2018 *International Encyclopedia of Intercultural Communication* emphasizes that when analyzing one's movement through the continuum, it is necessary to watch particularly for moves from minimization back to defense (645). However, much of the time the acceptance of difference in *Country* is clear. Mrs. Todd's acceptance of the eccentric Gen. Sant Bowden is a good sample of relational living. Beyond blood, Mrs. Todd accepts his grasp of military ritual, something beyond her experience and knowledge. More telling is the nameless narrator's acceptance of Joanna's self-isolation. Granted, the nameless narrator, in her writing quest, had earlier in the narrative sought a similar thing, but by this time in the plot she has grown relationally; she is different now, and her acceptance of ethnocentric behavior like Joanna's hermit existence advances her relational growth along the DMIS.

The next stage of Bennett's model would be adaptation, and Jewett's nameless narrator, a city woman on a quest to write in rural seclusion, adapts characteristics from her summer visit of Dunnet Landing. She exhibits an adaptive character when she shows signs of learning about Mrs. Todd's garden and her herbal remedies, adapting to life with Mrs. Todd. She exhibits an adaptive character when she recognizes the mourners in the funeral march early in the narrative, clearly adapting to and getting to know the community. As the novel progresses, so does the nameless narrator, who becomes more comfortable with boating and fishing, the strongest regional characteristics of the community. To be sure, Jewett's nameless narrator begins to adapt to so much from Dunnet Landing and its denizens that is difficult to pinpoint in Bennett's model where the adapting ends and becomes full-blown integration as if there could be a certain number of adaptations that mark a line in the sand where one is finally in that final stage of relational growth. For those who must have a climax, the Bowden Reunion and the communion with the eating of the pie is it.

As for the boundary between adaptation and integration, let us consider some final details from Jewett's *Country* in terms of integration. Let us begin by turning again to the scholars. Marcia

McClintock Folsom's "Tact Iis a Kind of Mind Reading": Empathic Style in Sarah Orne Jewett's The Country of the Pointed Firs" is an excellent essay in another important anthology on Jewett called *Critical Essays on Sarah Orne Jewett*, edited by Gwen L. Nagel in 1984. In her essay, Folsom describes integration in relation to tact, mind reading, and empathy. One who has these integrative characteristics is able "to reconstruct the whole through active interpretation of details ... to see into and beyond casual conversation, gesture, and expression, or details of houses, weather, and landscape, to identify the larger human significance of each small outer sign" (77). For Folsom, empathy is an integration in the mind. For instance, one morning the narrator awakens hearing Mrs. Todd in the garden, certain sounds are signs to the narrator that Mrs. Todd wishes her up and in the garden with her. These two are so integrated by this point that we are set up for the integration to come, a visit to Green Island where Mrs. Todd's mother, Mrs. Blackett, and her brother live.

This episode is loaded with integrative detailing. From the flag the brother William flies to communicate with fishermen to the more subtle communication between mother and daughter as the boat carrying Mrs. Todd and the narrator nears the island, Jewett provides much fodder for Bennett's DMIS. Far enough away still so that words cannot be heard, the mother on the island still knows that it is her daughter in the boat. Once on the island, the relating continues in a strong, growing integrative tone. Symbolically, Jewett suggests integration between the narrator and William when they bring a basket of potatoes to the house by hanging the basket on a hoe and each of them carrying an end of the hoe so that the hoe suggests an umbilical cord, much like Herman Melville uses a rope symbolically to connect Ishmael and Queequeg. A little later in the narrative, the nameless narrator adds, "Mrs. Blackett's world and mine were one from the moment we met" (73). And a bit later, the nameless narrator adds that she and Mrs. Todd's mother "understood each other without speaking," (81) marking the relationship with similar integrative prowess as seen between mother and daughter. Also on Green Island is where Mrs. Todd shares her story of lost love with the narrator, further evincing this integration. In fact, *Country* is so loaded with suggestive pastoral symbolism that a song sung by Mrs. Blackett and her son, William, becomes a symbol of their oneness, their integration. At one point in the performance, William "seemed to lend his voice to hers for the moment and carry on her very note and air" (80) when the mother's voice falters. Symbols of oneness and integration even take on an androgynous character during Mrs. Fosdick's visit in the episode right after the Green Island chapters. Here, Mrs. Fosdick relates a time when she had to dress as a boy and liked it. Part of Jewett's theme seems to be an integration of the male and female that is further enhanced by a city v. country pastoral theme.

As we near the end of the novel and the narrator's relational growth, we have the Bowden Reunion and the key episode with Elijah Tilley. On the ride to the reunion, everyone is making donuts so that even a donut becomes a symbol of integration and oneness. Among the various and sundry examples of integration during the actual reunion, none are as powerful as the narrator's consumption of the piece of pie with the word Bowden iced on it, serving as a kind of communion to represent the narrator's integration into Dunnet Landing. As Arnold Van Gennep asserted so many years ago, a shared meal is an incorporation ritual (20). In the final episode of the novel, the nameless narrator's accumulation of adaptions, her liminality, is recognized by Elijah Tilley, who, among other things, remarks about her fishing skills, and she is able to act like Mrs. Todd and particularly her mother when she is able to kind of read Tilley's mind, integrating or becoming one with him when nobody else in Dunnet Landing has been able to do that. So, in a sense, the nameless narrator has passed a course, taken her final examination with Elijah Tilley, and put into practice what she learned about relational living in her visit with him. The final image of *Country* portrays oneness and integration as the natural landscape and the town blend into one, "a golden chain of love and dependence" (121). Combine Jewett's use of the formal elements of literature with Bennett's DMIS, and we see a new way to learn from this classic novel of American Realism.

4

Satire and Insensitivity to Difference

The Problem in *The American* through the DMIS

The American appears in novel form and in English in 1879. Another edition appears in 1907, and James heavily edited it in the style of his more recent narratives. The following analysis will use the 1879 edition to show how Henry James satirizes the very topic of this book, sensitivity to difference. Every satire has a problem that it tries to perhaps fix or at least make people more aware of. The problem in *The American* is insensitivity to difference. The hero of *The American*, Christopher Newman, is in search of something, and Newman is similar to Ahab, if we replace the whale with Madame de Cintré, Newman's would-be trophy wife. However, Newman is also similar to Ishmael in *Moby-Dick* and, like him, encounters conflicts with difference outside of his native country. An analysis of a series of predominant experiences in this novel will show only superficial gain in sensitivity to difference by Newman, who at once seems open like Ishmael and closed like Ahab. The novel is a satire and focuses on the problem of insensitivity to difference. Using

Milton Bennett's DMIS, we can begin to understand why the problem exists.

We can also get a good idea of why James may have chosen to satirize the problem of insensitivity to difference based on his own life. Born in New York in 1843, James attended school in Europe, including Paris, the primary spatial setting of *The American*, and in 1875 settled for a year in Paris, and contracted to send columns back to New York for *The Tribune*. Though James had great experiences such as meeting Gustave Flaubert and Ivan Turgenev, his letters paint a different picture than one might imagine. Robert Emmet Long points to one such letter in which James "complains of his limited access to Parisian life, his failure to penetrate very far beyond the city's small enclosed American colony, and his columns in *The Tribune* continually suggest a spectator-outsider" (46). The description fits Newman.

Though James' satiric lens focuses on specific characters such as Newman, the satire does at times paint a broader picture. Newman, an allegorical name if there ever was one, is certainly representative of America and of an American. His vigor and toughness speak to the American frontier character, and his preference in the Louvre for copies over originals points to, among other things, American tendencies toward reacting, re-creating, making something better, seen more specifically in Newman's commercial prowess. Newman's power and individuality, quite evident when the young Madame de Bellegarde chastises him for not making alliances and operating solo on his quest to marry her sister-in-law, also speak to a more general American characterization. Throughout the novel, James drops lines that speak more to this general character. Newman himself seems to present himself as a typical American. Leon Edel writes of how much of that generalness stems from Newman's thoughts on how his acts evince "the privilege of being an American citizen" (197). This is part of the satirical problem. Many readers read Newman as a good guy. F.W. Dupee, who indicates about Henry James that Americans "in contact with Europeans was his fine unique theme," states that the conflict in James generally explored whether "rich self-made Americans were capable of the most delicate conduct" (96). Such a statement does not recognize that the conflict of sensitivity to difference is a two-way street. In *The American*, James is making fun of both sides of the pond. Edel writes that there's "comedy residing in the contrasting manners of American and Europe" (198). James' satire pokes fun at both. Both are insensitive to difference.

A close reading of the novel reveals how James, on a general level, satirizes both American and European character. As he does early in Chapter IV and often throughout the novel, James describes Newman's character in the general American term of democratic. It sounds good, but an insistence on equality can create a sense of the ascendency and superiority of sameness, marking those of difference as potential victims of ethnocentrism. In addition, if Newman is representative of the general American, then the general American, as James writes, uses the telegram rather than writing letters, illustrating the more practical and less abstract side of the American character as the telegram would be a more insensitive form of communication. This general sense of American practicality is further seen when Newman reflects that American youth "of twenty-five and thirty have old heads and young hearts" (139), emphasizing the rational and practical over the abstract, emotional, and he adds that French youth have the opposite general character composition. Newman's American friend Mrs. Tristram clearly differentiates the two sides in her diagnosis of why Newman was ultimately turned down from marrying Madame de Cintrè, describing their denial as "really aristocratic. They wanted your money, but they have given you up for an idea" (323). Newman's struggle with this difference is a crucial part of the conflict in the novel.

James uses phrasing throughout his novel that depicts these satirical generalizations of character. A good example would be the narrator's words "Like any other good American, Newman thought it as well not to truckle to the foreigner" (137). However, James also characterizes a general French insensitivity. Valentin, who, due to his sensitivity, is a kind of black sheep in the proud and hurting for money foremost French family in the novel, offers a description of Newman that shows he's not above insensitivity, especially with his own people, when he says that Newman "has not our confoundedly irritable French vanity" (138). Bennett would mark Valentin's dropping of the French side and embracing the characteristics of Newman and the American side as exemplary of reversal, seemingly shedding his own French skin in favor of this new American skin he's experiencing. Additionally, Valentin appears to accept but not necessarily agree with the American creed that time is money, asking after saying it and evincing his awareness with "Is that what you say in America?" (173). Almost all the characters in this novel seem to have some issue with sensitivity to difference, and James makes fun of them for it.

James even allows his omniscient third-person narrator to join in on the insensitivity parade and add to the satirical comedy. Perhaps one of the clearest ways *The American* fits within a context of Realism is through the DMIS. In the second sentence of the novel, the narrator presents an ottoman in the Louvre and then with some editorial omniscience adds that the ottoman "has since been removed, to the extreme regret of all weak-kneed lovers of the fine arts" (33). On the surface, the words appear to refer to those in need of physical rest from standing and walking; however, on another level, this authorial intrusion is ethnocentric in the sense that lovers of the arts are spineless. This sets the tone for irony and comedy, and James establishes this tone early in the novel, allowing his narrator these insensitive, defensive intrusions. Richard Poirier notes "James is only sporadically critical of Newman's incapacity to place himself in the position of others" (52). One of these authorial intrusions directed at Newman occurs, again, early in the novel. In the second paragraph, James' narrator criticizes Newman's cravat, but a few sentences later describes him as "a sufficiently promising acquaintance" (36). Newman is different because he wears his cravat differently, but he has the potential to fit in. At the start of the third chapter, James' narrator describes the Haussmann architecture prevalent throughout Paris to this day as having a "pompous sameness" (60), and at the end of the chapter it has an impassiveness. Clearly, James' satire waves the finger of insensitivity at both Newman for assuming he fits in and at the French, and especially, eventually, the Bellegardes, for being pompous when it comes to accepting the different Newman.

4. Satire and Insensitivity to Difference

Herein, James establishes his conflict of sensitivity to difference, ideal for a DMIS analysis.

In fact, once James establishes his conflict in terms of sensitivity to difference, his authorial intrusions fade away, and the rising action develops, loaded with a context open to Bennett's scale of measuring behavior. To be sure, if I had a nickel for every time the word *measuring* shows up in this novel, I could buy you a hamburger dear reader. Make that a cheeseburger. The editorializing voice intrudes once again near the end with a defensive denigration of religion, further cementing the negative tone around Madame de Cintrè's decision at the end of the novel to take the veil. After the first few chapters, the intrusions seem to step aside and allow the plot to unfold, and so much can be better understood using the lens of Bennett's DMIS. For instance, Bennett's model can be seen in the first two chapters; indeed, the first paragraph ends with the ever-practical Newman experiencing conflict with the abstractness of the art in the Louvre. To him, it is different. How he accepts the art is telling how he will accept French people, whom James has gone out of his way to differentiate from Americans based on ideas of practicality and abstractness.

By the end of the first chapter, Newman appears in the minimizing stage of Bennett's DMIS. Again, Bennett does account for fluctuation. Newman wants to be more relational and recognizes the importance of learning French. He admires Noèmie Nioche, a bad copyist who longs for something not unlike Ahab and Newman. One could say finding a sugar daddy and having a good time, being able to walk in the Louvre like one of the fine ladies she has seen so often before, is a kind of obsession or monomania with her. Newman's admiration of this young woman can be specifically seen in her English. Newman rationalizes that learning French would be helpful in his own quest and figures if this young Parisian woman can learn English, he can learn French. After all, he, too, has initiative, and it is that initiative that becomes the thing that he likes in her because it is in him.

A dialogue between Newman and an American he meets in the Louvre cements how the DMIS already has practical application to these early pages of the novel. Newman's friend is Mr. Tristram, an ethnocentric bore who primarily hangs out with other Americans and can only swear in English. At the end of the second chapter, he schools Newman on where to hang out in Paris, such as the Occidental Club where Newman "will see all the Americans" (55), and where to summer, Trouville, "The French Newport. Half the Americans go" (59). Though he views French as a splendid language, Mr. Tristram has made little effort to relate to the different culture. Newman seems to be farther along a more relational path in Bennett's scale than his friend who has lived in Paris for years but still appears to view his own culture as the only viable one while Newman, at least, appears to be accepting albeit only at a level that matches his universal worldview. The problem here is that Newman is still being insensitive to difference even, for instance, when he admires Noèmie Nioche's initiative. At a point in their dialogue Tristram exhorts Newman to change hotels to something more elegant. He thinks Newman must maintain a certain appearance, and when Newman insists his hotel is fine and that the staff is tripping over one another to accommodate him, Tristram assumes Newman must be exorbitantly tipping the staff, which Newman denies, adding an anecdote in which a worker brought him something and stood waiting afterwards. Newman offered him a chair. We may, perhaps, excuse Newman for this insensitivity so early in his visit, but a few lines later in his dialogue with Tristram, he reveals the purpose of his visit, "to see the world, … improve his mind, and … marry a wife" (51). There it is. Much like the irony, on the surface Newman appears a good egg, but his visit is a quest, a mission to marry, objectifying the bride as if she were to be a possession. Worst of all, Newman is unaware of how insensitive this quest is. Richard Poirier brilliantly points out readers read *The American* with a certain level of unawareness because we are entertained by the irony, the comedy. He writes, "Like Newman, we later see that in allowing ourselves to be entertained we had missed seeing enough" (28). Like *Romeo and Juliet*, *The American* turns from comedy to as much tragedy as satire can muster, most readers assuming a happy marriage at the end. Instead, readers are given a dose of harsh, grim reality that many will feel they should have seen coming, and it is Bennett's DMIS that helps highlight those predominant experiences in the novel that signal movement within the relational model. These experiences stand out under the gaze through Bennett's lens.

Several examples in *The American* illustrate this. In Chapter III we are introduced to Mrs. Tristram, and stages of the DMIS begin to jump off the page. Mr. Tristram has brought Newman to his residence, and the talk has begun on homesickness. Mr. Tristram would feed Newman's homesickness with the offer of warming up to their heater, an American amenity to their French home, while Mrs. Tristram feeds Newman's capacity for openness, accepting, and evolving down the path of Bennett's DMIS. She says to Newman, "you will soon get over your homesickness" (60). This feeds what Long describes as Newman's "illusion of limitless freedom" (57). The narrator describes Mrs. Tristram as not that attractive and one who has accepted herself as is, and she is curious to see how Newman might do trying to climb the social ladder of Paris, a skill that will require him to simultaneously climb Bennett's ladder of the DMIS toward being a more relational character. Since Newman has stated he is in quest of a worthy bride, Mrs. Tristram sets his sights on Madame de Cintré of the aristocratic Bellegarde family.

To get away from the sting of not being able to see Madame de Cintré, Newman leaves on a European tour that enables James to give us a brief episode of sensitivity to difference between Newman and a British acquaintance, a young Unitarian minister named Babcock. The fact that Newman here in Chapter V of the novel is hanging out with someone who speaks the same language is telling. The two have met traipsing about Europe. Mr. Babcock, who may be even more insensitive than Newman and whose insensitivity becomes one of James' most comic satirical targets, is so culturally insensitive that his "parishioners [had] gotten up a purse so that he may travel abroad, and thus improve his culture," and, to be sure, "he contributes to the sense of limited or restricted consciousness in the novel's characters" (Long 56). Mr. Tristram and Babcock have restricted views, but Newman's view appears to be limitless. James sets up the Newman and Babcock relationship by emphasizing they were "as different as possible" (106), and that is solely on relational terms, on sensitivity to difference. Newman accepts their relationship as traveling companions despite their difference, but Babcock struggles accepting the difference. Babcock secretly detested Europe. Newman accepted everything. Bennett would point out here, though, that Newman never goes beyond relativity to judgment, the key development if one is to move into Adaptation on Bennett's DMIS, and it is arguable that Newman's foot into the stage of Acceptance is tenuous. As their relationship as traveling companions comes to an end, Babcock asserts the two don't understand one another; their ways, as he will write in a letter to Newman later, are too different to reconcile. Newman counters with understanding doesn't matter. Newman may seem to accept, but Bennett would again point out that Newman struggles at the Minimization point. Newman struggles with his own self-awareness; moreover, he doesn't reconcile unity and diversity, for he could care less about such a reconciliation, seeing it as a waste of time.

When Newman returns to Paris from his travels around Europe, his relations with the Bellegardes is about to escalate. Mrs. Tristram has been to see Madame de Cintré, and Newman often visits the Tristrams. Early in Chapter VI, Mrs. Tristram reveals to Newman that Madame de Cintrè "suffers from her wicked old mother and Grand Turk of a brother. They persecute her" (119). Not ignoring the insensitivity to Turks, Mrs. Tristram's words show how restricted the Bellegardes are. Richard Poirier writes, "images of contraction and withdrawal ... invest every description of the Bellgarde family" (36). Though Mrs. Tristram tries to pass off the significance of honoring familial ties no matter what as a general French characteristic, she does have specific restrictive words for the Bellegardes. "With those people the family is everything; you must act, not for your own pleasure, but for the advantage of the family" (120). Mrs. Tristram speculates her friend is being forced into an arranged marriage. It has happened before. Before the chapter is over, James has Newman over at the Bellegardes, meeting Madame de Cintrè for the first time. It is an awkward time. Newman confesses to his trouble relating in Europe in general and Paris particularly, noting "one's point of view gets shifted round considerably" (126). The insensitivity of this statement further characterizes Newman's tendency to be defensive and/or minimalize, as he seems to really only be cognizant of his view, noting that there are these others out there, but if they interfere with his practical side, they are of little interest and less use. Ironically, Newman's first visit to the Bellegardes ends with Madame de Bellegarde, the matriarch of the family, asserting that she has been "the only person here capable of saying something polite" (132). That is debatable.

Poirier's wonderful comic analysis of the irony in *The American* deserves some attention within the context of Bennett's DMIS. Poirier describes the conflict in the novel as being "essentially between Newman's way of looking at life and Madame de Bellegarde's" (31). She is indeed the matriarch of the family, so it is fitting and proper that Poirier should focus on her. His description also places the conflict within the context of Bennett's DMIS that measures behavioral responses when worldviews collide. Poirier then further notes that the characterizations of Newman and Madame de Bellegarde "illustrate their permanent social differentiations" (40). The use of the word *permanent* is frightening because it suggests that one cannot change, and even though James fills his novel with plenty of predominant experiences that could mold and shape characters on a road toward ethnorelativism, nobody seems to learn much from these experiences. Again, this may be the strongest element of Realism in *The American*, for as Poirier writes, "there is nothing that can be called development in characterization. Instead of it there is only dramatic intensification of the differences between the categories" (50). The categories would be the open Newman and the closed Bellegardes.

Despite Newman's openness, limited as it is, he begins the novel as an outsider in Paris, and he is still one in the end, shut out by the Bellegardes, who barely let him into their lives. But it was long enough to get both Newman's and the reader's hopes up that he and Madame de Cintrè would wed in the end. Newman appears to be on the threshold of moving into another social level as well as another level of Bennett's DMIS; however, he never really budges. If anything, the harsh, grim reality of the climax points to more realistic, practical living from Newman. Long likes to write about how close Newman came, writing James "has chastened Newman's consciousness and introduced him to the inner life. Newman's abnegation of self at the end is a 'correction' of his exaggerated American sense of life as being wholly outward, the will limitless, the self absolute" (157). Newman refuses in the end to exact revenge on the Bellegardes for their role in closing the door to his marriage to Madame de Cintrè because it is not practical; it is not good business. Newman embraces his American commercial character. Donald Weber sums up Newman's situation quite well, writing, "Despite his professed desire to abide by the 'proper forms,' Newman's lack in the eyes of the Bellegardes, of appropriate 'foundations,' his thin personal history, and his failures in etiquette doom his American quest; Newman is indeed 'the outsider' in a modern anthropological-sociological sense" (728). Newman had trouble understanding why he has been rejected because he cannot adopt the worldview of the Bellegardes, but he ultimately decides to burn the one piece of evidence with which he could potentially blackmail the Bellegardes. Making the French family uncomfortable by holding his evidence over their heads has to do until Mrs. Tristram in the last words of the novel informs her friend that the Bellegardes were likely not frightened by the possibility of Newman blackmailing them because they considered his American character and that it wouldn't change, which is why we laugh a little when the very last words of the novel have Newman taking a glance at the fire to see if his evidence that he could hold against the Bellegardes has burned up.

Newman is no role model for sensitivity to difference. The novel is a satire after all. Some close readings of some of Newman's actions and words throughout the narrative would serve well to illustrate just how satirical the novel is. The early chapters are telling in this regard; in fact, the first scene is telling. Newman is trying to broaden his horizons; however, he is unprepared, something this book could have helped him with. He doesn't know good art and offers to buy a bad copy of Bartolomé Esteban Murillo's *The Immaculate Conception* done by Noèmie Nioche. She scratches her chin baffled by the offer. She knows it's no good. In pressing to buy it, Newman exhibits relational skills when he considers he may have offended the copyist somehow, but he is still pressing, foreshadowing his monomaniacal mind ala Ahab, for when Newman sets his mind on something, the process of obtaining whatever it is looks rather obsessive. Edel writes that Newman has "predatory aspects" and a "vulgar streak of materialistic self-satisfaction," and that he's "boorish" in "his belief that anything can be bought" (196). Furthermore, as the opportunity to reach his goal seems to fade, he laments that the young copyist doesn't know any more English, defensive within the DMIS for a worldview that sees English as the only viable language and minimizing in that sharing that language would be something Newman would like about her but only because it's his language. Newman has learned some French and uses it during this scene, one of the reasons, along with the comic tone, that we may get sucked into the ideal of Newman achieving his quest and the novel ending with a happy marriage before reality shatters that. The comedy like the relational elements at work in the novel both set us up to want to believe, much like Ambrose Bierce sets us up with his fantasy of escape from the hangman's noose in *An Occurrence at Owl Creek Bridge.*

There is still much to be mined from the very first scene of the novel to further reveal how Bennett's DMIS can help us understand relating to difference. We are introduced to his name here, Christopher Newman. One can't help from seeing Christ in there, which suggests Bennett's ultimate relational character, the liminal one, like Ishmael. The allusion also conjures up ideas of insensitivity to difference toward the liminal one. The Bellegardes could be Christ-like to Newman's Romans. Then, there's the last name, Newman, and he is trying to become a new man, easily put into context with Bennett because Newman wants to be more ethnorelative, but he is bad at it. To be sure, as Long puts it, Newman's consciousness "is not highly developed" (59). Sometimes it can be good to try to understand a thing by what it is not, which is why this satire by Henry James works well in explaining how we can measure sensitivity to difference in characters from great American novels, even when they are satires.

So, Christopher Newman only appears to be sensitive to difference, but it is still enough to suck us into his quest. Take, for instance, still in that first scene mind you but after Noèmie Nioche's father has arrived, when Newman's optimism about the father, who has suffered loss, getting back on his feet again, strikes the father as insensitive; however, Newman does not read this. He minimalizes by suggesting that all are the same when it comes to getting on one's feet again after a loss. It is also defensive within Bennett's framework because Newman, again, sees his own worldview as the only viable one. The Nioches, though, seem to pick up on to the fact of his one-track mind and take advantage of that, the father offering French lessons, which Newman accepts. His acceptance again forces us to think of him as becoming more relational, but during this talk, he describes French as something not spoken but chattered.

As the Nioches leave and James turns to his second chapter, the action remains in the Louvre, and Newman is on to his next quest, another kind of mini-quest or sub-quest within the realm of his ur-quest, which will ultimately become the desire to marry Madame de Cintrè. First, though, another painting catches his eye, Paolo Veronese's *The Wedding Feast at Cana*. In a wonderfully comic understatement the narrator tells us that, to Newman, "it satisfied his conception, which was ambitious, of what a splendid banquet should be" (45). Newman doesn't seem to have a clue how to be sensitive to difference because he has all these preconceived notions in his head about the way things are supposed to be. He is thinking about making another, though better, bargain with a male copyist of the Veronese when his process is halted before he takes action by the arrival of an old friend; however, nothing will seemingly stop Newman and his questing spirit. Scholars continue to write about this. In 2015, Páraic Finnerty writes of Newman, "for him, she [Madame de Cintrè] is a rare artefact from a private European collection who will be all the more rarer within the American marketplace" (36). Yes, she is like one of the paintings in the Louvre. Newman is mired in Bennett's defensive and minimization stages of ethnocentrism within the DMIS because he is so damned independent, is so lacking in self-awareness about his insensitivity to difference, and is unable to reconcile unity and diversity.

The old friend who interrupts his quest of the Veronese copy is none other than Mr. Tristram, and the early times of their rekindled relationship further paint this picture of insensitivity to difference in James' satire. Newman immediately begins measuring his old friend, using their handshake to take the defensive position that there was "a want of response in his grasp" (46). Newman only thinks these words, but he does verbally denigrate Mr. Tristram, questioning his manhood in asking about his use of a parasol, something apparently not in his worldview of men. They then begin discussing the concept of copying great art, a discussion that takes on symbolic heft within the context of sensitivity to difference. The art in the Louvre can represent French high society, the society into which Newman wishes to integrate. However, Newman prefers copies of great art rather than the great art itself, signaling how he really doesn't care for French high society. Furthermore, integrating is a kind of copying. The copyist must move in and out of different artistic styles, extending empathically to represent great works of art from varied artists. A visitor such as Newman presents himself as a copyist, willing to move in and out of French high society, but he is a bad copyist of French high society much as Noèmie Nioche is a bad copyist of great art. He claims to Mr. Tristram that he hopes the paintings in the Louvre are originals because he doesn't "want a copy of a copy," and Mr. Tristram replies that the copyists are very good and "imitate, you know, so deucedly well ... you can't tell the things apart" (48). Newman will never reach this integrative point on Bennett's DMIS scale, and a big part of James' satirical problem is that Newman thinks he can and cannot see how his character is mired in Bennett's lower stages of sensitivity to difference.

Newman's blindness to his insensitivity is wonderful dramatic irony, but may be too wonderful as others also fail to see it, including scholars. F.W. Dupee writes, "Newman is so perfectly self-satisfied that he can afford to be open-minded" (98–99). The thing is that Newman is not really open-minded. Once he and his old friend leave the Louvre, they go to the Palais Royal where Newman seems fixated on the women nursing their infants, something, again, out of his worldview. He ends up telling Mr. Tristram his story since they last met in America. James describes it as "an intensely Western story," adding a little later of Newman's character in the story, "a more completely healthy mortal had never trod the elastic wild of the West" (52–53). Newman may seem ripe for growth, but he is unprepared, and his worldview is at odds with the one in which he has put himself. A couple of months before this action in May 1868, Newman had an experience in which he overcame a grudge, a revenge, and in fact was so disgusted with his insensitive thoughts that he felt he had to get away. Newman is in a financial position in which he can do this. However, he has no idea what he is getting into and should be disgusted with his own insensitivity. For instance, at the end of Chapter II, he expresses how he would like to be introduced to the crowned heads after Mr. Tristram offered such a meeting as a joke. Newman simply doesn't get it.

After Chapter II James moves his plot along toward Newman's interaction with the Bellegardes, the relating that will be the remainder of our focus in this study of *The American*, and it is a visit at the home of the Tristrams the day after the meeting in the Louvre that sets the novel on this path. Mrs. Tristram has some relational issues; however, she bonds with Newman and comes to realize he admires her despite his peculiar relational manner with women. Newman thinks little of her husband, who strangely appears stuck in Bennett's reversal stage of the DMIS when he denigrates his home country, the United States, but doesn't really accept France either as he tends to hang out with other Americans in American venues. In contrast, Newman praises the United States as the greatest country while accepting every proposal Mrs. Tristram organizes to visit with someone. This Philadelphia woman who has been in Paris for eight years helps Newman to know Europe and accept the forms and ceremonies, but he ultimately reveals to her that it's a trophy wife he's after. Newman says things such as "I want to take my pick. My wife must be a magnificent woman" (70). Or, "there must be a beautiful woman perched on the pile, like a statue on a monument.... I want to possess, in a word, the best article in the market" (71). James is making fun of Newman because he is going about relating all wrong although he thinks it's all right. The satire becomes more clear when viewed through the lens of Bennett's' DMIS. Bennett's undifferentiated other in Newman's quest for a bride is in a kind of beauty pageant. Mrs. Tristram describes Newman's desire as insatiable, and this is how Newman becomes like Ahab. Newman's American individuality and sense of equality drive him on his quest. He claims to have no prejudices in the search although he concedes it would be nice if she spoke English. Newman is not extending himself empathically and remains in the ethnocentric stages of Bennett's DMIS.

Newman has learned some French, but this is only useful for the quest, which begins in earnest after Mrs. Tristram offers Madame de Cintrè as the object of his desires and sets him on his way to the Bellegardes where it is easy to tell right away which of them may be open and which may be closed. Upon arriving at the Bellegardes, Newman meets Valentin, the youngest son, who takes Newman's card to take to his sister whom he has said he believes to be in; however, before he gets to the door, the older brother appears, takes the card, and announces that she is not in, and there you have it. The older brother will act ethnocentrically toward Newman while the younger brother will be more open and empathic. Newman thought of this younger brother as the butler until he learned better. Valentin, as Poirier points out, is the man who, for Newman, "translates Urbain's [the elder brother] snobbish insinuations into language plain enough to expose their potential vulgarity" (42), eliminating any doubt as to the elder brother's sensitivity to difference regarding Newman.

It is at this point in the narrative that James takes Newman on the European tour where he meets Babcock, although there is a chapter devoted to the subplot of the Nioches in between, and these pages provide ample evidence of how Bennett's DMIS can help us better understand the way these characters are relating. Newman is again clueless, insulting the French youth in general for not courting Noèmie Nioche in a manner more consistent with his worldview, which Mr. Nioche depicts as "not the ideas of this country" (85). Mr. Nioche is there for Newman's French lesson, and even that Newman turns into a practical experience. This scene is a good one to illustrate how James gives some characteristics of Newman that makes readers lean toward him being open and authentically relational. James adds at one point how "Newman took an interest in French thriftiness and conceived a lively admiration for Parisian economics" (88) as evinced by the wheeling and dealing of the Nioches. This interest is more of an amusement, though, to Newman, for he will never accept such financial doings himself as his life must be lived on a larger scale. Newman is also an amusement for Noèmie Nioche, who butters him up by complimenting him on his French, which has improved. She and her father are playing Newman although he is unaware. He is also unaware that Noèmie Nioche has very little talent for painting or that the work he has asked of her is impossible, his unacquaintedness coming to light in predominant experiences in almost every chapter of *The American*. Noèmie seems to want more even early in the novel, and Mr. Nioche clarifies their want of money for a dowry; however, these kinds of arranged marriages in Europe do not meet Newman's worldview, leading him to declare that such behavior is a kind of social disease of which there have only been a dozen cases in the entire history of the United States, such a superior place in Newman's measured ranking.

Newman finally gets to meet Madame de Cintrè, her first name, Claire, clearly continuing the allegory, and shortly after she becomes the most highly measured prize on the continent to Newman. He is particularly smitten, in another instance of minimization, with her excellent English. Still, she seems closed in the way she looks and what she says, expressing, for example, that she doesn't travel much. He appears open, extending his legs in a habitually symbolic gesture ala Dimmesdale covering his heart; however, again, Newman's gesture should be read as his comfortableness in who he is, unwilling to change, a key climax within the formal structural elements of almost any narrative and key to Bennett's DMIS and moving into more ethnorelative behavior. Valentin is also at this meeting, but his presence only brings out more of Newman's ethnocentricity when his inexplicable grinning makes Newman think, "Damn his French impudence!" (126), showing Newman also a kind of source for amusement to him.

Roughly a week later, Valentin visits Newman and strikes up a friendship. Evidence of reversal surfaces during the first visit. Valentin lets on that part of his attraction to Newman is "he has not our confoundedly irritable French vanity" (138). He also shares that he lives under his mother's rule and admires Newman's independent spirit. Upon subsequent visits, the friendship grows and seems exemplary of Bennett's relating in the upper more ethnorelative scales of the DMIS. James portrays it thusly: "No two companions could be more different, but their differences made a capital basis for a friendship of which the distinctive characteristic was that it was extremely amusing to each" (143). There's the amusement factor again. Also, note the use of the word *capital*. This is not relating on a level in which different worldviews are adapted. The different worldviews here are a means of entertainment. Each man remains in his character. There is little change. Newman isn't moving, and Valentin maintains his occasional reversals, indicating how Americans such as Newman have the advantage of having not debauched themselves and are less prejudiced, clearly seen at the end of Chapter VII when Valentin lets on that his sister would never lower herself to visit Madame Dandlard, the woman Valentin and Newman visit at the end of the chapter.

Valentin also lets on some details about his sister during the time spent with Newman. Valentin reveals her previous arranged marriage and how marriages in his family have almost always been more or less arranged for social reasons, and we already know how Newman feels about those. None of this registers with Newman, who meanwhile has been visiting Valentin's sister. Newman in time discloses to Valentin his desire to marry his sister, Madame de Cintrè. Valentin speaks of the great difference between them and that such a union is very unlikely. Newman will not accept marriage to her as impossible, and in pressing forward with his quest, amuses Valentin with the possibilities of such a courtship. These two may appear to be accepting one another, but they are not. Newman only wants Valentin's help in marrying his sister, saying to him, "You come into my programme" (163); however, Valentin is no better. He says, "it will be very entertaining. Excuse my speaking of it in that cold-blooded fashion, but the matter must, of necessity, be for me something of a spectacle. It's positively exciting. But apart from that I sympathize with you" (161). Such sympathy is about as much given to the animals in the zoo. *The American* is a satire in which neither side of the pond will come away as sensitive to difference in spite of trying to seem that way, and that is part of the relational problem that James explores in the novel.

In the next chapter, Newman proposes to Claire, Madame de Cintrè, and it becomes clear that Newman views her as a thing. To him, she seemed "rare and precious—a very expensive article, as he would have said, and one which a man with an ambition to have everything about him of the best would find it highly agreeable to possess" (165). Now, Newman's quest zeroes in on her, and during this meeting she seems to sense what is going to happen. Valentin praised Newman to her the night before, and, evincing his ethnocentrism, after Newman becomes aware of the service, he denigrates him to Madame de Cintrè's face, calling Valentin "a noble little fellow" (167). Newman's ethnocentrism toward the French worldview represented by the Bellegardes also becomes clear during this proposal. The differences between the Bellegardes and Newman are summed up by Newman based on what Valentin told him, and that is the Bellegardes stand "somehow on a higher level," an idea Newman states he does not accept (168). He does not see the difference. Poirier writes, "while we see in the comedy the essential and profound differences between Newman and the Bellegardes, he sees only those differences which might be explained away" (41). That is his problem, and James satirizes it; however, James satirizes the Bellegardes, too. Poirier again is instructive, writing "it is no wonder that the social comedy in the novel invariably involves the exposure of different kinds of European unreality" (53). Poirier's diction is key. He states that some of the problems James satirizes on the European side are untrue. At the end of the proposal chapter, family pressure on Madame de Cintrè is front and center, existing as a cause for her not to marry Newman. However, most scholars are quick to point out, and James admits it himself in a later edition of *The American*, that the Bellegardes would've jumped at the chance at Newman's money.

Newman and Claire agree on a six-month period in which marriage will not be discussed; however, discussions now arise between

Newman and the matriarch of the Bellegardes. For Madame de Bellegarde, being an American "is simply not an imaginable part of her world" (Poirier 38). Each side in this relating is mired in the lower stages of Bennett's DMIS. The eldest Bellegarde son, the allegorical Urbain, is in agreement with his mother, who sums up the idea of this courtship in the rather realistic terms of "I would rather favour you, on the whole, than suffer you" (191). Now, the conflict rises high as Newman and the Bellegardes represent two different worldviews that struggle with sensitivity to that difference, the main thrust of James' satire, matching perfectly with Bennett, who emphasizes how conflict concerning sensitivity to difference is "created from differently contexted experience" (38). James at this point in his narrative is also able to intertwine this major conflict between Newman and the Bellegardes with the subplot involving the Nioches and bring both together within a relational context and sensitivity to difference.

Most of the comedy in this rising action stems from the dramatic irony of Newman not realizing how the Bellegardes are treating him. Newman "is too spontaneously and innately superior to be able to recognize the evidences in social conduct of contrived and devious nastiness" (Poirier 36), and the superiority is part of the satiric problem because Newman, in thinking of himself in such a way, prevents himself from accepting other worldviews. Over the next several chapters, we see Newman's French has not really improved much. His lessons with Mr. Nioche are all but abandoned; however, James does not abandon the Nioches from his narrative, and, when he brings them back, he brings in Valentin Bellegarde to meet them and mix his plots. James stresses how they shake hands differently in meeting Mr. Nioche, but it is his daughter, Noèmie, who takes center stage by stealing Valentin's heart. He seems smitten by her from the start. Newman's interests have focused on the father, but Valentin calls him a "seedy old gentleman" (201) and thus begins his infatuation with Noèmie Nioche, which she feeds. Long recognizes "just as Noèmie's self-assertion victimizes Valentin, Newman's victimizes Claire" (61). Through the next several chapters both main plot and subplot run similar conflicts. Valentin's openness toward Newman and ultimately Noèmie Nioche hasten his death in a duel over Noèmie, and Claire's openness to Newman to even consider marriage leads her to a living death of the cloister as a Carmelite nun rather than sully her family name. The satire relates, again, to a kind of dramatic irony, for Newman doesn't seem to realize the damage his questing spirit has caused nor how this spirit has spread to Noèmie Nioche. Long writes how she "becomes a kind of parody of Newman's early values ... the assumption that the world exists to give pleasure to one's self" (61). Unfortunately, these are not simply early values of Newman's.

James provides little evidence in the second half of *The American* of Newman progressing toward the more ethnorelative stages of Bennett's DMIS. Urbain is "disagreeable to him ... a man towards whom he was irresistibly in opposition" (207). "The idea of having this gentleman mixed up with his wooing and wedding was more and more disagreeable to him" (210–211). The Bellegardes have given Newman permission to court Madame de Cintrè, but Newman does not care for the elder brother or the mother; moreover, he continues to view Madame de Cintrè as an object, James characterizing her as "a marble goddess" in Newman's eyes (223). Newman attempts to be civil around Urbain and Madame de Bellegarde, but unlike them, he cannot maintain control of himself, his independent spirit fierce. His insensitivity to the Bellegardes has Newman "indulging in an unlimited amount of irresponsible inquiry and conjecture," finding "himself confronted by the conscious ironical smile of his host" (227), a further irony, though, that appears lost on Newman. Newman's inability to adapt is not lost on Claire, who notes how he finds Valentin an amusement, how he "would not like to resemble him" (234). Further along in this crucial conversation, Claire further notes how Newman does not like her mother and older brother, Newman adding to her agreement that they don't like him either. Bennett reminds us that acceptance does not mean agreement, and despite the lack of agreement between the Bellegardes and Newman, there is enough acceptance. Claire declares her love for Newman, and the wedding is on. Newman's insensitivity to difference goes to another level after this.

4. Satire and Insensitivity to Difference

Bruce McElderry summarizes well Newman's insensitivities after there is a marriage agreement. The first of Newman's social mistakes that McElderry lists is Newman sending telegraphs to American friends about the wedding before a formal family announcement. Next, Newman proposes to give a ball before Claire's family can (46). James tells us "Newman knew that the marquise [Urbain] disliked his telegrams, though he could see no sufficient reason for it" (251), and Mrs. Tristram warns Newman to let the Bellegardes play this out their way; however, Newman continues to act insensitively. James shows us Madame de Bellegarde's response to Newman's party plans. "I can't think of letting you offer me a fête until I have offered you one" (253). Newman appears blinded more than usual now that his quest has reached a point in which he can say to Valentin, "I knew what I wanted, exactly, and I know what I have got" (266). James takes Newman's self-satisfaction to great heights before letting the satire take care of this problem. Even to Claire, Newman repeats the word "coveted" and says, "You have been holding your head for a week past just as I wanted my wife to hold hers. You say just the things I want her to say. You walk about the room just as I want her to walk. You have just the taste in dress that I want her to have. In short, you come up to the mark; and, I can tell you my mark was high" (271). This is classic minimizing on Bennett's scale, for Newman makes no reference to liking anything about her that is different. Everything has already existed in a preconceived notion.

Now, as Newman appears poised to integrate into a higher society different than his, Valentin looks to be on the verge of stepping down the social ladder into the very different society of Noèmie Nioche. *The American* is satire, and it is Realism. Neither of these men's imagined ideals are going to pan out. Before Newman can expand his grand ethnocentric plan to Valentin and convert "his bright impracticable friend into a first-class man of business" (299), Valentin gets mixed up in a duel over Noèmie Nioche. This drama provides yet another aspect of French culture for Newman to denigrate. Valentin presents the duel as French custom while Newman thinks of it as barbaric. As Bennett reminds us, acceptance does not mean agreement, but that does not condone denigrating diction.

Again, *The American* is Realism, and none of this ends well. Before Valentin is mortally wounded in his duel, Newman learns that the Bellegardes have changed their minds. The marriage is off. The Bellegardes see no insensitivity on their part. Newman is furious. Claire enters a convent. Valentin is dying, and Newman must go to him. With him, his mind on Claire, Valentin, more empathic than the American, recognizes trouble on Newman's face. The news of the marriage being off and Claire entering a convent compels dying words from Valentin meant to help Newman. There is a Mrs. Bread, long time English caretaker in the family, who has some dirt on the family. Seems Madame de Bellegarde refused medicine to her husband, effectively killing him over a dispute about an arranged marriage for Claire with an older man. We already know how Newman feels about the custom of the arranged marriage, but now with this additional information, Newman has the opportunity to capitalize and win Claire back and have vengeance on the Bellegardes. There is significant difference between the elder Bellegardes and the younger ones. Paul Italia identifies the difference, writing, "The senior Bellegardes (matriarch and eldest son) feel free to use patricide, usurpation, incest, and pandering to preserve their power, while the younger Bellegardes cut themselves off from life by invoking the duel and the cloister to preserve their vanishing honor" (365). That is the Realism of *The American*. Both Long and McElderry write about how Newman rises above by not exacting his revenge, but as Mrs. Tristram remarks at the very end of the novel, the Bellegardes counted on Newman's character. Their confidence in Newman not going through with his threats to reveal the dark family secret and ruin them guided them. They appear to have understood Newman better than he them. We can learn a lot about sensitivity to difference from these relational mistakes in James' satire.

THREE

The Twentieth-Century Novel
Invisible Man
and *For Whom the Bell Tolls*

5

Invisible Man
An Existential Liminality

The narrator of *Invisible Man* is an invisible man, living in an abandoned forgotten basement. He's a writer. He wrote this book, *Invisible Man,* about how he got to this point. His journey takes us through episodes riddled with intercultural sensitivity theory meshed within the formal elements of an existential novel. In the end, through writing the novel, the narrator attains a kind of liminality, more clearly than that attained by Ishmael, an existential liminality that may manifest itself most clearly in the novel when the narrator says he will fight back against Dr. Bledsoe, the Black head of the college the narrator ultimately gets thrown out of. Dr. Bledsoe says "go ahead, go tell your story; match your truth against my truth" (141). It is here where the narrator recognizes an existential relativity to truth, which beckons the need for liminality, which will come out when the narrator indeed tells his story.

In his book, *Basic Concepts,* Milton J. Bennett writes, "there are different boundary conditions" (8) to consider when applying his Developmental Model of Intercultural Sensitivity. It is all over Ralph Ellison's *Invisible Man.* Nathan A. Scott writes, "the book is packed full of the acutest observations of the manners and idioms of human styles" (114). The narrator experiences many differing world-views, propelling him up the DMIS toward ethnorelativism. Ellison, in fact, emphasizes imagery involving lines and up and down movement. These patterns mimic the stages of the DMIS with sensitivity to difference being measured on a scale that has ethnocentrism at the bottom, ethnorelativism at the top, and lines marking stages of relational development along the way. The narrator of the novel often refers to a dividing white line. Depending on which side of the line he's on, the narrator must relate differently because on one side he's relating with his Black brethren and on the other side with the White man. The first time he mentions the white line, he positions himself as one who must toe it, keep his eye on it, for if he were to cross it, he must know that he now has to act differently. Arthur P. Davis notes that in the novel there are "two worlds," one of segregation "not yet dead" and one of integration "not fully born" (606). As Ellison emphasizes the imagery of the line, the characterization suggests a character who moves back and forth across a line from one world-view to another. The fact that Ellison raises the difficulty factor of this kind of crossing over, this connection, this integration throughout the episodes of the novel reveals his existential leanings, which is why this particular twentieth-century novel lends itself well to an analysis pointing toward an existential liminality (*limen* in Latin, by the way, meaning threshold).

The narrator's episode with Mr. Norton illustrates the existential angst of crossing the line. Mr. Norton is a powerful White man and a founder of the all–Black college the narrator attends. He has arrived on campus, and the narrator is to drive him. The narrator is eager to do this. However, as Roger Rosenblatt writes, "it was his efforts to make himself seen" that "got him into difficulties" (197). Ellison's irony can be cruel. In the car together, the line has been crossed. While driving, the narrator tells us, "Half-consciously, I followed the white line" (45). He seems to wish to remain in both worlds and not move too far into the White world, leaving his old world behind. However, it would appear that line has already been crossed, and difficulties arise. This is what John S. Wright calls "Ellison's syncretic drive to combine, reconcile, and reintegrate competing cultural realities" (155). During the drive, they come across the cabin of Jim Trueblood. The narrator muses: "How all of us at the college hated the black-belt people, the 'peasants' during those days! We were trying to lift them up and they, like Trueblood, did everything it seemed to pull us down" (47). Lifting them up means making them more like the White man, making them, in Bennett's terms, accept, adapt, and integrate. The pulling down points to keeping relations with one's own kind and having an ethnocentric view. The narrator has accepted the White worldview. He has entered a college designed to assimilate young Black Americans, helping them adapt to the different worldview, the White worldview. The narrator's episode with Mr. Norton is a rare crossing of the line in reality, not in classroom theory, and the results, especially after they stop to speak with Trueblood, are a hard real-world existential lesson for the narrator.

The most existentially troubling thing about the visit with Trueblood is what it leads to, although the visit itself creates an existential angst because, among other reasons, the visit should have never happened and is crazy. Trueblood ultimately finds himself speaking to Mr. Norton about the White man cutting down the successful Black man. In another movement, Trueblood has crossed back into his worldview and denigrates the White worldview he was on the cusp of entering into at the start of this conversation. Whether it's the shock and awe of Trueblood's words or the heat Mr. Norton is not used to, the man the narrator is in charge of, and is responsible for, seems to be having some kind of episode. It appears to be something with his heart as he asks the narrator for some stimulant, specifically mentioning whiskey. At this point, Ellison's narrative takes an absurd turn as the nearest place to purchase some of this precious elixir is at a fine establishment down the road called the Golden Day, which just so happens this day to have been run over and taken over by a platoon of "crazies" from a local institution. The most telling scene within this bizarre episode for furthering this text in its context of sensitivity to difference is at the very end. An educated, traveled veteran, a man who has experienced several worldviews, though not all real, talks about the educated Black narrator going up relationally with the White man but down relationally with the Black man. In

Bennett's terms, the narrator exhibits reversal because of his preference for the White worldview. It is as if there are two DMIS models, one for relating with Blacks and one for relating with Whites. The narrator has moved into the ethnorelative stages of the White DMIS but is in the ethnocentric stage of reversal with the Black DMIS. He seems to be masked in both, making this one of the first instances in the novel of liminality. The vet says that the college has made the narrator "a walking zombie," "invisible," "the most perfect achievement" (92) of the college's design; however, Ellison characterizes the narrator more marginalized here. Attaining liminality does not happen overnight as Joseph M. Armengol writes that the narrator will go through a process of invisibilization, which is "linked to the parallel visual metaphor of blindness, which Ellison, unlike Melville, uses to describe the racial biases embodied by both black and white characters" (36). Yes, to be sure, Melville tends to focus on the blindness of Capt. Delano in *Benito Cereno.* Delano is blind to the fact that a mutiny has taken place, that Black slaves have overrun a Spanish slave ship. Ellison's narrator will run into both Black and White characters who will not see him as he is as the various predominant experiences unfold in the narrative, molding and shaping the narrator. The positivity of liminality will have to wait for the end when the narrator becomes a writer.

For now, the narrator realizes that this episode is going to get him kicked out school; it has been in Bennett's sense a conflict that can be seen as a predominant experience, molding and shaping his sensitivity to difference and relational growth. A new worldview looms on the horizon. But, for now, there's only existential absurdity. The narrator had tried to follow the line and be the Black White man, but look where it got him? He is forced now to find a new identity after "shunning all but the straight and narrow path that" (97) the college had put him on, that horse where he straddles two worldviews. But the White worldview would never really let the narrator integrate, and the narrator was taught to accept that. He thinks of the superficiality of his crossing the line and now comes to understand that it is dangerous for Blacks to cross the line. This hearkens back to classic Black poetry such as Paul Laurence Dunbar's

5. Invisible Man

1895 "We Wear the Mask" as well as the color line written on so eloquently in 1903 by W.E.B. DuBois in *The Souls of Black Folk*. The narrator understands that he has actually been wearing a mask when entering that White world. From the point of view of Dr. Bledsoe, the Black head of the college, the narrator was a bad actor who had forgotten how to lie when crossing the line into a White worldview, asserting an existential superficiality to the relating.

The novel never strays far from these existential and relational roots so in tune with Bennett's DMIS. A couple other beautiful examples follow. First, when the narrator is in New York with his last sealed envelope containing Dr. Bledsoe's damnation of the narrator rather than a recommendation, he has a poignant moment of line crossing. The son of the man to whom the narrator is to deliver the letter has intercepted the letter, opened it, and read it. He has sympathy for the narrator. His name is Emerson. We should not neglect the allusion to the nineteenth-century American prophet of oneness and integration who asserted time and again that everything is connected to everything else in his true Transcendental fashion. The young Emerson is conflicted over revealing the truth about the letter. He asks the narrator, "do you believe it possible for us, the two of us, to throw off the mask of custom and manners that insulate man from man, and converse in naked honesty and frankness?" (182–183). The disillusionment the narrator experiences upon understanding the truth about the letters again advances the existential notions in the novel as well as furthering the importance of sensitivity to difference. In a final glowing example, there's the work of the Brotherhood in the latter part of the novel. Many readers think of them as Communists. Whatever label is given, they are trying to relate to the people of Harlem, trying to get them to accept and adapt some of their ideas. However, their "work had been very little, no great change had been made" (433). The narrator noticed in time that they are failing, failing to get the people to move up Bennett's DMIS to the higher relational stages with the White worldview and subsequently cementing the sense of existential futility.

If we examine more closely some of the formal elements of Ellison's novel, we expand the horizons of both Bennett's DMIS and how it plays with the text as well as the existential themes that tend to keep characters from moving too far up in the relational stages of Bennett's model. Bennett writes about predominant experiences that mold and shape relational growth. Within the formal elements of literature, these are conflicts. The narrator experiences a conflict his first day in New York City. He runs into difference. He runs into Peter Wheatstraw, a city version of Jim Trueblood or the vet at the Golden Day. The narrator should know better, but is drawn into his madness for a few pages before pondering, "God damn, I thought, they're a hell of a people! And I didn't know whether it was pride or disgust that suddenly flashed over me" (174). The narrator's conflict involves a relational choice that he cannot settle on, reaffirming he's becoming liminal as he maintains both worldviews. One of those views is that he is proud to be Black. The other is Bennett's reversal, for the narrator accepts and adapts a White worldview that denigrates Black people and exhibits a defensive posture. The conflict later in the novel with the Brotherhood's response to the narrator's speech reinforces the role the DMIS plays in Ellison's plot structure and enhances the existential side to the narrator's relational growth. The Brotherhood holds a view that their style to win over the people to accept their views must take a reasonable, scientific approach. The narrator's speech is much more instinctual and wild, so the Brotherhood does not accept the speech. They denigrate it and suggest the narrator needs more training in conforming to their worldview of this style point. James Millichap sees dark, fell purpose behind such action, writing "if the integrated Brotherhood seems much different than his segregated college in many obvious ways, it ultimately proves another construction of the majority culture designed to keep its Black minority in its proper place" (136). The existential absurdity of this discussion is that the narrator's speech seems to have been rather successful in getting the people interested in the cause of the Brotherhood.

The conflict the narrator experiences early on in New York City allows for the element of setting to play a role in how Bennett's DMIS works in *Invisible Man*. The city works almost like an antagonist similar to the arctic of a Jack London story or the ocean in Stephen

Crane's *The Open Boat.* These naturalistic stories are replete with existential motifs such as repetitive actions coming to nothing and trouble trying to find any essence or meaning behind what is happening to them. The naturalistic setting seems poised to destroy any character in its path. The city setting of Ellison's novel seems poised to destroy not so much the narrator's life but his relational skills, particularly evident in the episode with Mary, another allusion. She is a saint. She accepts difference. She takes in the narrator after his episode at the paint factory left him, among other things, lobotomized and walking so weakly in Harlem he has fainted. After a sleep, Mary exhorts the narrator to try not to get corrupted by the city, which could keep him from growing like her to become characteristic of someone high in the relative stages of Bennett's DMIS. Yet, the narrator will resemble Walt Whitman in that he ultimately accepts everything. Whereas, Mary would be more like Ralph Waldo Emerson in that she will not accept anything that she deems corrupting. By accepting the views that come to him, the narrator is able to build a wide liminality in himself, making him a rainbow coalition of all the difference he has integrated into his life.

This is probably why *Invisible Man* has a good share of symbols that communicate liminality. For instance, even when Ellison writes that the hungover narrator's head was splitting from a loud noise early in Chapter 15, we know better. The narrator has just assumed a new identity with the Brotherhood, a new worldview he puts on like another layer of clothing. The splitting in his head points to the different views incorporating him. Tony Tanner recognizes that the narrator must struggle with the conflict that the way the Brotherhood identifies him is with their own terms, ethnocentrically, but that the narrator feels there is more to his identity (41). This is the layering of liminality in the character of the narrator, and Ellison lays it on thickly throughout his novel. Why there's even liminal symbolism in Tod Clifton's paper doll toy. Clifton has left the Brotherhood and is witnessed by the narrator hawking the toy on the street. The paper doll is attractive because it appears to move on its own, but there's more to it than meets the eye. The narrator comes to understand an invisible thread, controlled by the holder and connected to the doll, makes the doll dance. Symbolically, this doll is the narrator, and he has several threads, each attached to a different worldview. Not all of Ellison's symbolism illuminates liminality. He has more traditional symbols, too, such as Brother Tarp's chain; however, even that resounds with a worldview that is part of the Black experience that can be viewed as just one worldview within a Black man such as the narrator. The chain is a simple reminder not to forget that worldview, that that worldview is a part of who he is, symbolizing the denial of slavery.

Elements such as character and point of view are covered naturally since *Invisible Man* has first-person narration; there is a final word about the tone of that narration that can shed new light onto the existential liminality of the novel. As one might suspect, irony is at the root of most of this existential liminality. For example, the narrator and Brother Wrestrum have a disagreement over the chain that Brother Tarp gave to the narrator and which the narrator now has resting on his desk. The symbolism of the chain as a part of Black experience bothers Brother Wrestrum because it represents a part of the characterization that he wishes not to be there. The wish is reminiscent of the psychological denial seen in *The Scarlet Letter*, but even more telling within Bennett's DMIS is the minimization inherent in Brother Wrestrum's view, as well as that of the Brotherhood, and Communism by extension. Brother Wrestrum says, "we want to make folks think of things we have in common" (383). The irony of acceptance being exclusive must not be lost. The existential absurdity of Bennett's minimization chips away at the noble goal of the Brotherhood trying to get the people to accept them so that they can help them. Their own acceptance of the people they want to be accepted by is limited to be sure.

Liminality leads to many ironic situations in *Invisible Man*. A clear example of Ellison sustaining this ironic tone can be seen when the narrator is mistaken for Rinehart only apparently because of his hat. Actually, he's mistaken for Rinehart by a woman on the street and decides to increase his integration into Rinehart's skin by buying a wide hat in Rinehart's style. This simple adoption of the hat makes the narrator Rinehart in the eyes of many. He muses, "It was as though by dressing and walking in a certain way I had enlisted in a fraternity in which I was recognized at a glance" (474). Who knew liminality could be so easy? But, it's not, is it? This irony is comical, but more seriously we see the narrator near the end of the novel stating that he "was never more hated than when [he] tried to be honest" and "never been more loved and appreciated than when I tried to 'justify' and affirm someone's mistaken beliefs; or when I've tried to give my friends the incorrect, absurd answers they wished to hear" (559–560). This is the kind of existential irony of relating that makes one marvel that we are able to cross lines and accept, adapt, and integrate with those who have different worldviews, and thanks to Ralph Ellison's *Invisible Man* and Milton Bennett's DMIS, we can learn how to get better at it.

The novel affords ample opportunity for students to become exposed to multiple behaviors and important concepts Bennett addresses in his essay, "Becoming Interculturally Competent." Of note in Ellison's novel is the notion of acceptance not meaning agreement. In *Invisible Man*, the White world is viewed by most of the Black characters in the novel as different and humanly important, but not on a very sensitive level. One strong example occurs early in the Mr. Norton episode. The narrator is driving and flattering Mr. Norton. Ellison's narrator says, "it was advantageous to flatter rich white folks" (38). The narrator fantasizes about such behavior leading to anything from a big tip to a scholarship. He has crossed the line into this White man's world and accepted a rather capitalistic value within the worldview of a rich White man. That is the only point of agreement, the capitalistic value, nothing remotely higher minded, more relational about accepting difference than to make a buck. In another example, similar to the corruption admonition associated with the setting from the saintly Mary of Harlem, the advice from the vet, the same one from the Golden Day on the bus heading north, helps the narrator, just kicked out of school, to better understand that the line can be crossed and one can enter into the White man's world, but must not adapt. The White worldview is viewed as largely corrupt. The vet advises, "Play the game, but don't believe in it…. Play the game, but play it your own way—part of the time at least" (151).

The latter counseling points to only superficial steps into acceptance since that is safest. Adaptation should be limited, if possible, and the narrator should try to create a kind of new version of himself to exist in this new world. This is another level of liminality in *Invisible Man.*

This counseling also adds to the conflict, for the counseling, the advice, the message from his schooling at the college was to accept, in sharp contrast to the vet's advice. To show how much the narrator has grown, he refers to those college days as an Eden as he stands on the cusp of expulsion. True, it was an ideal, unrealistic. He's having an existential revelation about ethnorelativism and its limits for him. Dr. Bledsoe's scolding on the Mr. Norton episode about taking "white folks where we want them to go" and "showing them what we want them to see" (100) points to those limits. In his essay, Bennett writes about authenticity and adaptation. He urges that acceptance of difference must go beyond relativity to judgment and that adaptation must be authentic. Dr. Bledsoe's final words, unlike those the narrator had previously heard at school, unveil a masking behind acceptance. The vet advises an act when it comes to adaptation.

The application of this seemingly sound advice is pervasive in the novel. Even the Black professors at the college must don chauffeur's caps if they intend to safely drive by themselves around the campus and town. Back at the Golden Day, the vet talks about how his time in France made him forget about acting, clearly suggesting World War II–era France as more ethnorelative when it comes to race and sensitivity to difference. There is, to be sure, a marked ethnocentrism of Blacks toward Whites in the novel, most conspicuous with all the experiences the narrator has had when crossing into the White world. Nathan A. Scott writes of Ellison's narrator, "he has tried all those things by means of which it would seem that [he] might achieve visibility in American life" (113). It is no wonder he becomes defensive when relating to Whites. He gets to a point reminiscent of the Black experience in Langston Hughes' "Harlem," in which the death and denial cannot be taken anymore, leading to an explosion; or as with the American colonists, who felt they could no longer negotiate with King George III and further felt they were at the point of war with Patrick Henry's words: "Give Me Liberty or

Give Me Death." After being lobotomized after the plant explosion at Liberty Paints, the narrator expects nothing from the White side of the line. Yes, the relational stance in *Invisible Man* resembles Black Nationalist ideology that one might find in Malcolm X or Ta-Nehisi Coates. Jim Crow is alive and well in *Invisible Man.*

For the narrator, though, the novel is alive with what Bennett calls predominant experiences, all seemingly negative from the narrator's point of view as described in these previous pages, but he still grows relationally, reaching Bennett's heights of liminality. Moving to New York City, for instance, is a predominant experience for the narrator. Early in his time with the Brotherhood, the narrator, unnamed like Jewett's to promote liminality, lists like chapters in a book some of his predominant experiences that have set him on the liminal path. He lists the college, the hospital at the paint factory, and the battle royal that I still need to address. And, now early in the Brotherhood, he writes, "I was becoming someone new" (327). The liminality in the novel becomes existential through the relativity of truth, lessons learned by the narrator during the episode in which he is often mistaken for Rinehart, blurring set identities, leaning toward liminality and the existential truth of the indeterminateness of truth. Within existential philosophy, cultural sensitivity theory, and Ellison's novel, this is all good. We want liminal people. *Invisible Man* has a part where liminality is associated with good leadership. Brother Hambro warns of the Brotherhood becoming too one-sided (scientific, rational) in its approach. He shrugs saying, "if you go too far in that direction you can't pretend to lead" (494). The pretending refers to the actor in this case juggling multiple scripts, multiple worldviews. Interestingly, in 1993, Janet M. Bennett noted Barack Obama, at the time noted for being the first Black elected president of the *Harvard Law Review,* as the epitome of, at the time, what intercultural sensitivity theory was calling constructive marginalism. Now, we think in terms of liminality with her words. "In some ways, Obama presents us with an ideal case study of a man in the middle of many cultures. While various cultural groups may each seek his allegiance, he appears to claim for himself an identity that is beyond any single cultural perspective" (Bennett 110). Then, he became leader of the free world. Ellison's voice in this novel leads, too, and the path leads to liminality as a litmus test for leadership. Ellison emphasizes writing the book as a strong relational move. The narrator feels it late in the novel. "I felt that somewhere between Rinehart and invisibility there were great potentialities" (499). The book.

The book is loaded with key passages that illustrate the existential liminality that Ellison's narrator achieves and shares to the world in the book. In an interview with Allan Geller in a 1964 *Tamarack Review*, Ellison speaks of the sensitivity to difference in the writing and that part of his, and the narrator's, job as writers "to try to write so truthfully and so well and eloquently about a specific background and about a specific form of humanity that it amplifies itself, becomes resonant and will speak to other people and speak *for* other people" (20). The first of some early key passages that exemplify this existential liminality involves the definition the narrator gives for hibernation in the Prologue. The hibernation refers to his basement dwelling. The definition goes, "A hibernation is a covert preparation for a more overt action" (13). Again, the book calling for liminality is the overt action. The narrator does not nihilistically resign himself to meaninglessness, meaning action is meaningless. The narrator's marginality is a kind of liminality. In *The Ritual Process*, Victor Turner notes how liminal/marginal individuals are linked with authorship (111). Scott, again, is instructive in his remarks about how Turner would view Ellison's narrator, writing, "What Turner is most eager to remark, however, is the wrongheadedness of regarding liminality as a merely negative state of privation..., for it is precisely amid the troubling ambiguities of the liminar's *déclassment* that there is born in him a profound hunger for *communitas*" (115). In writing his book, the narrator takes on an existential work ethic of the likes of Dr. Rieux in Albert Camus' *The Plague*, who carries on in his absurd existential world. Ellison's novel and his wonderful narrator give us the same.

A good example of that absurd existential world would be with Dr. Bledsoe's words when he's reprimanding the narrator. Not only do his words have an existential tone, but they further communicate how Bennett's DMIS enhances our understanding of relational behavior within the scope of his model. Dr. Bledsoe says, "I'll have every Negro in the country hanging on tree limbs by morning if it means staying where I am" (141). In this insensitive remark, Dr. Bledsoe claims he will adapt the ruthless tactic of lynching as performed by racist mobs and private associations such as the KKK. Additionally, this is at once a declaration of reversal, favoring the worldview of the different culture over his own, as well as denial by the flat-out murder. A little later he denigrates ideals such as pride and dignity in favor of a darker power that he adapts from Whites. And, in the end, Dr. Bledsoe's reprimand precedes a cruel set up in which the narrator is dismissed from school but with sealed letters of recommendation that in reality are far from recommendations.

After being kicked out of school, the narrator has more predominant experiences in New York, experiences with which he can grow in sensitivity and see the possibilities of being integrated with others. Ellison alludes to Ralph Waldo Emerson in an important scene worth revisiting when the narrator is at an office for an interview, wielding the last of the seven letters of recommendation that Dr. Bledsoe has convinced him to keep sealed so that he doesn't see that Dr. Bledsoe is denigrating him rather than recommending him in the letters. The last interview is with a Mr. Emerson; however, it is his son who meets the narrator, opens the letter, and opens the door for the narrator to see that his conflict with his identity is meaningless in a relative world in which liminality reigns, except apparently in the one-sided White world of the elder Emerson, a world the younger Emerson is not accepted in because of his liminality, seen in his ability to integrate with the narrator and try to help him look more deeply into the world the narrator wishes to enter. In another allusion, Ellison likens the two to Huck and Jim from Mark Twain's classic novel. Similar to those two, the narrator mistakenly journeys deeper into enemy territory. The narrator winds up at Liberty Paint, known for the whitest white paint, and like a fortune made off of slave labor, the narrator's job is to make the paint that white of whites. There's an accidental explosion, and the injured narrator is whisked away to the factory hospital, where he is shocked and lobotomized, seemingly for practice. The level of denial the narrator is experiencing in this White world is cruel and inhuman. Out of the vast whiteness he awakens to after the operation, the narrator cannot recall his name. Now, he can truly create his own reality as an existentialist and his own identity as one who adapts from others. In his characterization of the narrator, Berndt Ostendorf has the narrator adapting "ethnic pluralism and diversity" as a writer though "a marginal or transitional position requires a special vision and a special talent for interactions," called a double vision that "implies an acceptance of dialogue and of a plurality of voice" (150–151). Having adapted things from his previous predominant experiences, these early New York ones continue the narrator on a path to existential liminality and becoming a writer.

The narrator begins to dress in another layer of worldview a couple chapters later in Ellison's novel when he mixes with the Brotherhood. As mentioned earlier, this group is often thought of by readers as the Communist Party. Their recruitment of the narrator stems from them witnessing his oratorical skills, something he has shown before in this narrative. He is told by them that he will now "emerge [as] something new" (285), meaning the narrator will have adapted to a new worldview, a view that becomes a little clearer only a few pages later in chapter 14. It seems the Brotherhood sees the narrator as the next Booker T. Washington, and what do we remember of him? His legacy in terms of sensitivity to difference reveals a man who integrated into White society. The Brotherhood's strategy is to make change within the system. Theirs is not the violent overthrow of the likes of Ras the Exhorter, who would be more representative of a separationist approach similar to the Black Nationalism espoused by Malcolm X, for instance, in the 1960s. The Brotherhood would be more like Martin Luther King. They want the narrator to work for change in the Black community by playing the White man's game, which means more liminality for our narrator as he will anew the need to adapt to some different worldviews in order to become the leader they want him to be. They want to create a leader who will make White leaders like him because he will remind them of parts of themselves. This is Bennett's minimization at work. The narrator has a new identity and new name with the Brotherhood. He isn't even supposed to write home, but home is still there in the liminal man he is becoming.

The speech hotly debated by the Brotherhood receives analysis from our insightful narrator, and his own analysis of his own speech further illuminates his existential liminality. His own analysis recognizes "What had come out was completely uncalculated, as though another self within me had taken over and held forth" (344). All the predominant experiences in the narrator's amazingly full life mold and shape him. The different worldviews that he has encountered and which he adapted, enabling him to integrate at times, are a part of him not unlike Ernest Hemingway's code hero who comes up next. Hemingway code heroes are able to live in the moment because they have such a vast repertoire of experience that they are able to act without thought, creating a seamless integration with life itself thanks to liminality. The narrator seems to have had a similar experience giving the speech. He adds, "Even my technique was different.... I *was* someone new" (344). He credits the success of his speech to an integration that occurred with the audience while speaking. He was truly living in the moment. Later near the end of the same chapter, the narrator tells us how "on the way to work one spring morning I counted fifty greetings from people I didn't know, becoming aware that there are two of me" (371), but a few words later he concedes that there are more sides: "my grandfather and Bledsoe and Brockway [from Liberty Paints] and Mary" (371). Each of these and more go into making the narrator liminal. Scott explains the narrator's liminal character, writing, "the definition of the world, as he has discovered, is possibility—the very infiniteness of which may be defeating," (113) but the narrator is not defeated. He carries on, creating his own reality. He can live in liminal moments in which he's able to switch worldviews depending on the circumstances.

Tod Clifton's disappearance, odd reappearance hawking the toy doll, and murder are a big part of the narrator's existential liminality within Bennett's DMIS. As the narrator questions some of Clifton's decisions, he minimizes his relationship with Clifton, thinking Clifton should've been thinking like him. But this questioning by the narrator allows the life and death of Tod Clifton to be a model of existential liminality. Clifton adapted a different worldview, choosing a kind of anonymity not unlike the hibernation the narrator himself will undertake to write his book, which he is able to do if we think of it as *Invisible Man*. Writing has become linked to an attainment of liminality, and Victor Turner notes that, for those such as Ellison's narrator, a society "emerges recognizably in the liminal period," and it is "characterized as an unstructured or rudimentally structured and relatively undifferentiated ... community" (96). Tod Clifton may have entered a liminal period after disillusionment with the Brotherhood. He fits into the kind of liminal character Victor Turner describes, writing "these persons elude or slip through the network of classification that normally locate states and positions in cultural space" (95). The existential realization that accompanies liminality may be a rite of passage for the likes of Tod Clifton and the narrator. Turner writes, "Liminality implies that the high could not be high unless the low existed, and he who is high must experience what it is like to be low" (87). The narrator has experienced lows. Yet, though he has had his share of predominant experiences that are existential, the narrator is fortunate to have not suffered the worst, an absurd pointless death such as Tod Clifton's at the hands of the police. Yes, there is Black ethnocentrism in the novel with the likes of Ras the Exhorter, who denigrates the narrator like Malcolm X denigrates Martin Luther King, but there is far more White ethnocentrism in *Invisible Man* as seen with the police brutality and death of the now-martyred Tod Clifton.

Despite the denial on the part of the Brotherhood, who want the narrator to think in one narrow way, the narrator expands his relational horizons and sensitivity to difference in some of the final key passages in the novel. The experience in which the narrator is misidentified as Rinehart multiple times cannot be over emphasized in the context of liminality. Our reflective narrator, looking back on that predominant experience, understands fully "you could actually make yourself new" (488). In the context of liminality, new means a new character who is able to adapt to a new world view. This is, again, the existential living in the moment, since existence precedes essence. Existentialism, turns out, is not only productive for its work ethic but can produce better relating as well. When one's relating tends to be controlled more often than not by outside forces that turn out to be false and absurd, one finds oneself in an existential existence. The narrator notes near the end of the novel how each of these outside forces were "attempting to force his picture of reality upon me and neither giving a hoot in hell for how things looked to me" (497). With such denial, no wonder individuals such as the narrator create their own realities in true existential fashion since there is no established one, and furthermore these individuals similar to the narrator are able to sift through the variety of worldviews they encounter and adapt as necessary, creating a liminal mind, and promoting that liminality through writing. W.T. Lhamon, in his book *Deliberate Speed,* describes the narrator's writing as showing "people how to admit their differences" (51). John Callahan, in his book *In the African-American Grain,* describes the narrator at the end of the novel as one who is no longer an orator but a writer who has a better "awareness of diversity and complexity" (183). Again, if we think of Ellison's *Invisible Man* as the book the narrator creates, the book does indeed promote sensitivity to difference.

In the final scenes with Ras the Exhorter, Ellison almost sets up a juxtaposition of worldviews not unlike Jewett does within the structure of her novel. In the end Ellison puts side by side an ethnocentric view and an ethnorelative view. Turner puts this conflict in a liminal context, writing, "It is as though there are here two major 'models' for human interrelatedness, juxtaposed and alternating" (96). Like Malcolm X, Ras shouts for no more Uncle Toms, seeing their adaption to the White worldview as destructive to the Black's freedom and equality. He sees the narrator as a pawn, convinced into accepting and adapting to views of the Brotherhood in a Bennett act of reversal against his own culture and worldview, seemingly preferring another over his own.

But Ras has a singular view whereas the narrator is able to see multiple views at work, how he was played to reach the people and how Ras has been played to now kill the narrator. Because the narrator does not adhere to a singular worldview but rather accepts multiple worldviews, he is open to existentially and sensitively recognize in those differing views "the beautiful absurdity of their American identity and mine" (547). The narrator sees that now, and his book can help others to see, too. Nathan A. Scott is again illuminating when he writes, "in his liminality, Ellison's young knight does not choose merely to pour scornful laughter on the social establishment … he remains totally in earnest" (117–118). Scott adds, "Ellison's protagonist is a liminar who, though separated from the established orders of the world, is not yet estranged from himself" (119). Perhaps, though, Ellison's narrator says it best, "I knew that it was better to live out one's own absurdity than to die for that of others" (547). So, within spring imagery of rebirth, signaling a new coat to the narrator's rainbow coalition of worldviews, he puts on the garb of writer and unlike the singular ethnocentric view of Ras the Exhorter exhorts readers to accept a liminal world in which everyone is connected to everyone else, virtually eliminating difference. Ellison's Romantic language is Whitmanesque as he writes, "there is a *death* in the smell of spring and in the smell of thee as in the smell of me" (567). Not only does this echo Whitman's bonding of us in a liminal individualism by every atom, but it echoes Wallace Stevens and his assertion that death is the mother of beauty. The death of one worldview due to a predominant experience does not eliminate the worldview; it is simply replacing it with the new one coming from the new experience. In the ethnorelative individual who is open to accepting, adapting, and even integrating into different cultures and worldviews, accumulating worldviews furthers his ability to live in the moment in an existential liminality.

This growth begins with the first chapter after the Prologue. Chapter 1 is often anthologized as *Battle Royal.* It is a self-contained chapter with a beginning, a middle, and an end. Nathan A. Scott describes the early narrator as Van Gennep might. He is a "neophyte [who] first undergoes some detachment or dislocation from his established role in a social structure or cultural polity—whereupon he finds himself as a novice in a 'liminal' situation in which he is neither one thing nor another, neither here nor there, neither what he was nor yet what he will become" (115). What he is to become is a liminal writer writing about liminality. The situation in *Battle*

Royal is that the narrator finds himself in an unfamiliar White world in this chapter. He was to speak at some entertainment that some White men have created, but he ends up in the *battle royal* part of the entertainment, a free for all as the title suggests, White men watching Black youth beat up one another. The narrator must adapt. He does, but for the duration of the chapter's rising action, which is to say most of the first chapter, that outcome is in doubt. He survives the experience and can now chalk it up as one of Milton Bennett's molding and shaping predominant experiences, an experience that is at once liminal and existential. It is liminal because he has adapted and integrated, however roughly, into a different worldview for a time. It is existential in that the action is absurd and meaningless, but the existentialist takes the experience to heart. In *Either/Or,* Søren Keirkegaard writes that the liminal, existential man "discovers now that the self he chooses contains an endless multiplicity, in as much as it has a history, a history in which he acknowledges identity with himself" (220). That identity is whatever identity he chooses. When liminal, there's a choice, which is so existential. So, from the point of the *battle royal* forward the reader experiences the continued liminal and existential growth of the narrator that culminates in *Invisible Man.*

6

Robert Jordan
and the DMIS

A Literary Model
for Intercultural Sensitivity

Yes, from the ancient sacred texts came calls for civility, for sensitivity toward others. From the selfless service of the *Bhagavad-Gita,* to the call of the Tao to be sensitive enough to live in the moment, to Socrates and Plato pointing out the folly in following the crowd, and the Bible emphasizing in Matthew that one should take the strait gate, spiritual texts have through all time addressed the ethics in relational issues. John Donne, a metaphysical poet if there ever was one and ordained a priest by the Church of England in 1615, wrote in "Meditation 17" that "no man is an island" (617). Three hundred twenty-five years later, Ernest Hemingway's *For Whom the Bell Tolls* hits the bookshelves, the title and epigraph acknowledging Donne and "Meditation 17," for Donne's writing also reads "any man's death diminishes me, because I am involved in mankind, and therefore never send to know for whom the bell tolls; it tolls for thee" (617). Hemingway's secular text has as much punch concerning relational living. The central character of the novel, Robert Jordan, is a sensitive man, a civil man with a code of behavior. He can be called a Hemingway code hero, and Jordan's code marks him a good literary model when it comes to being sensitive toward others, particularly those of difference. To make it easy, we have our model, Milton J. Bennett's Developmental Model for Intercultural Sensitivity, to gauge the model character of Robert Jordan, enabling readers to know what to look for as they experience Hemingway's characterization of Jordan.

I was preparing for a study-abroad course called *Hemingway's Cuba* when I first became enamored with *For Whom the Bell Tolls.* According to Fidel Castro, the book was a philosophical model for an existential guerrilla revolution. At the time, I also saw the possibilities with Robert Jordan as a model of intercultural sensitivity and integration, and an analysis of the novel under the gaze of Milton Bennett's DMIS reveals just how much we can learn about intercultural sensitivity from Hemingway's novel about a civil war, perhaps the epitome of an attempt at integration, or genocide; furthermore, in this particular case, one side, the Socialist side, even suggests political theory driven toward integration through economic equality. There's a lot to talk about regarding this novel and issues of sensitivity to difference. Other Hemingway scholars have addressed the idea of Robert Jordan having an integrative character, but none have been able to chart character growth from ethnocentrism to ethnorelativism without an instrument, which is why Bennett's model is key here one last time in *The (Un)Welcome Stranger* as it creates a way to gauge.

Not long after the 1940 publication of *For Whom the Bell Tolls,* critics began addressing Jordan's civility and sensitivity. In 1953, Stanley T. Williams noted how Hemingway's connection to Spain stems from the author's experiences during the Spanish Civil War (134). Many would argue the golden rule of writing is to write about what one knows. Hemingway makes clear on the first page of his novel that relating is linked to understanding. Jordan begins the novel well beyond ethnocentrism. Jordan later states, "I know this country from before the movement" (24). Jordan loves Spain. He knows the region, remembering the gorge of which Anselmo, his guide to the guerrilla camp, speaks. Hemingway knows Spain, and he knows his character Robert Jordan will integrate more efficiently and effectively while in Spain if he can enter Spain with some knowledge about Spain, similar to what we did with our students in preparing them for that study abroad in Cuba, and similar to what anybody can do to better relate to difference.

To be sure, literature can provide readers without the benefit of having previously visited a region with what Philip Young in his seminal 1966 study states Hemingway provides Robert Jordan, "handy knowledge. Right at the start Jordan is able to get the confidence and admiration of his fellow guerrillas by showing that he knows a great deal about their horses, simply by glancing at them" (109). Earlier in his book, *Ernest Hemingway: A Reconsideration*, Young describes Robert Jordan as a character who makes working "adjustments" (80), and it is Bennett's DMIS that will help us chart them. For instance, that same region that Jordan symbolically integrates with by lying "flat on the brown, pine-needled floor of the forest" (1) has experienced changes since Jordan was last there, and he is certainly not totally omniscient. So, it is no wonder that Anselmo leads him to camp on a trail discernible to Anselmo but not to Jordan, who accepts Anselmo as his guide. Neither is it no wonder that the young American cannot recall the mill, but he adjusts, or, as Bennett would say, adapts, accepting the difference and learning, remembering. Near the end of the novel, Karkov, the *Pravda* journalist who has read Jordan's book on Spain, notes how Jordan has "a great way with the Spaniards" (425). But don't simply take another character's take on Jordan when Hemingway himself lays out how Jordan thinks about relating to a Spaniard. "If you knew Spanish he [the Spaniard] was prejudiced in your favor, if you knew his province it was that much better, but if you knew his village and his trade you were in as far as any foreigner ever could be" (135). So much of the novel addresses relating to difference, and it all starts with knowing as much about the difference as possible, before even arriving at the place, especially if you're trying to integrate into it.

In the 1970s and 1980s, scholarly criticism from Robert Stephens and Edwin Stanton stand out as continuing to explore Robert

Jordan's relational character but, again, without the benefit of a bona fide model like Bennett's to guide us into a clear, well-lit place where we can see Jordan's sensitivity. Still, Stephens illuminates the discussion with his 1972 essay, especially when he addresses an early adjustment Jordan makes. Stephens notes how Jordan, despite his previous experience, is a college professor and soldier who comes from a realistic point of view, and that he is entering in these mountains a region inspired by the magical. In a clear example of Bennett's adaptation, Stephens writes about how when Jordan first enters camp, he recognizes the different mindsets, the different worldview, and adjusts and adapts by dismissing "that political world known through discursive, dialectical language [for] an embracing of a magic and mythical world known through the language which creates it" (155). A good example would be the silent, first dinner. As Arnold Van Gennep asserts in *The Rites of Passage*, a shared meal is basically an incorporation ritual (20). Hemingway writes, "They were all eating out of the platter, not speaking, as is the Spanish custom" (22). Jordan adapts and integrates, and he is good at it. In *Basic Concepts*, Bennett writes that one trying to integrate ought "to become sensitive to the *feeling* of appropriateness that accompanies a different worldview in an almost intuitive way" (20). Jordan is so good because of his preparation and experience, becoming that Hemingway code hero who knows almost intuitively what to do in so many situations. Jordan is not unlike an artist or more cognitively complex individual, positioning him in a good place for developing intercultural sensitivity.

Stephens further asserts that in the novel there is "a growth of a sense of community within the partisan group" (157). The early cave scene is essential to understanding the relational level of the novel. Anselmo educates Jordan on how cautious one must be trying to relate to Pablo, the leader of the guerrilla gang. Jordan demonstrates relational knowledge by offering cigarettes, joking with the gypsy, and offering him absinthe. He uses all these things to appease the tension created by the awareness of the dynamite he carries for their mission to blow up a bridge. Other than Pablo, everyone in the cave also benefits in a relational way by being united by the cause for which they fight, a military integration that Hemingway later characterizes like a communion or the experience one has in the presence of great art. Jordan's adaptive character in relating to the gypsy particularly interests Stephens, emphasizing Jordan accepts the gypsy despite the gypsy's level of seriousness not being at a level Jordan would prefer. Jordan also struggles with Pablo's wife, Pilar, particularly with her palm reading. Bennett rings the bell that there can be acceptance without agreement and that, in fact, there should be to avoid the pitfalls of relativism. The philosophical discussion near the middle of the novel about predestination, a talk primarily powered by Andrés, one of the guerrilla soldiers, reveals a metaphysical difference between Jordan and the others.

A beautiful case of Jordan's ethnorelativism shortens that distance. Jordan points out to Anselmo a link "between gypsy and American Indian beliefs in man's brotherhood to bears," and, in the same conversation, Jordan adapts again, showing another link between the two, connecting with Anselmo's point about gypsies not ethically challenged by killing outside the tribe (155). Despite Jordan's invective toward Native Americans when searching Pilar's bed, Stephens notes Jordan's knowledge of this lore, adding that Jordan has an "extra sensitivity ... to such psycho-cultural patterns [gypsy lore] because of his travels and study in Spain" (153), which is exactly what great writing can do for the student preparing to travel abroad, the expat, members of multinational teams, educators, health care workers (Bennett, *Basic Concepts* 71–74), or the neighbor trying to connect to neighbor. We can learn about sensitivity to difference from Hemingway's novel, and students will not be under the pressure Robert Jordan is experiencing, significantly limiting such outbursts as when searching Pilar's bed. We can learn a great deal from the positive steps Jordan takes toward intercultural sensitivity.

Stanton's 1989 book further maps out Jordan's sensitivity, more readily perceived now through the lens of the DMIS. He indicates how Hemingway knew the setting of his novel, having "traveled the Guadarrama Mountains on foot, on horseback, and by motorcar" and how Hemingway infused his central character, Robert Jordan, with prior knowledge of the region as Jordan "has been fighting for the Republic since the beginning of the war, has traveled all over the peninsula for years, has written a book on Spain, and is an instructor of Spanish at a university in Montana" (152–154). Consider when Jordan goes to the camp of El Sordo, the leader of another guerrilla gang. When he first meets El Sordo's guard, Joaquín, the guard accepts Jordan because Jordan knows about bullfighting, the guard's hometown, and Jordan empathizes with him over the murder of the guard's family. Bennett writes in *Basic Concepts,* his "DMIS suggests that a lot of attention should go to preparing trainees to experience another culture before trying to train any particular behavior" (71). Earlier in his book, he writes. "cultural knowledge becomes a doorway into the embodied experience of another culture, allowing us to respond to cues with the same kind of 'unconscious competence' that we use in our native cultures" (62). This is Hemingway's code within the DMIS. To be sure, we all can improve our own openness to cultural difference by reading great books that address the regions we are visiting, not necessarily to the extent of Robert Jordan, but using Bennett's DMIS can help as we note a character's acceptance of difference. Literature fits into an objective culture study, but it is to be studied not to learn so much about the culture but about the process of becoming ethnorelative (Bennett, *Basic Concepts* 7). We have a model character for Bennett's model.

Stanton, similar to Stephens, points to the mountain setting being moral, and Jordan, who has an empirical character, accepts this way of thinking and opens himself to the mystical (62, 101). Though both the rational and empirical camps would claim they hold truth, most would agree that the empirical side is more associated with certainty since knowledge for them is more rooted in the senses. Hemingway's novel associates certainty with bigotry. Jordan must be open. For instance, consider the metaphysics of a sublime interconnectedness of people. Hemingway does do this during a conversation tinged with Romantic Socialism that takes place after Maria, a young woman the gang rescued from fascists, kisses Joaquín. Maria states she kissed him as a brother and tells him "I love thee and thou hast a family. We are all thy family." Then, Pilar adds that Jordan is family, too, and Jordan accepts this saying to Joaquín "we are all thy family" and, later, "all brothers" (139). Stanton even suggests a feminine pastoralism, advancing the relational character of Hemingway's novel by emphasizing Jordan's acceptance of Pilar, palm reading, at least, excluded, and his ultimate integration of sex with Maria, which is affirmed, again, by Bennett in *Basic Concepts* when emphasizing connection is not so much cerebral (44). Their linking suggests further linking, of Protestant and Catholic and Anglo and Hispanic. However, it is with a focus on the body that Stanton further writes, "By giving him Maria, Pilar enables [Jordan] to learn the mysteries of the senses, the body, sexuality. Then Jordan is fully accepted by the Spaniards as a member of the band, while he feels himself more 'integrated' with the world" (167–174).

To emphasize how important following custom is in this setting, Hemingway gives us material to analyze with the gaze of intercultural sensitivity. A good place to look would be the short conversation between Fernando, another of the gang, and Pilar that takes place after Fernando witnesses Jordan kissing Maria the first morning. Fernando argues that such kissing is very inappropriate or insensitive, denying Spanish custom; however, Pilar saves the day by adding that Jordan is Maria's "novio" (92), appeasing Fernando and custom, creating acceptance. In another conversation a few chapters later, Pilar converses with Jordan, recognizing that she never really took Maria from him, stating, using the affectionate and highly suggestive appendage "rabbit" for Maria, "I give you back our rabbit" (156). A little later, Jordan asserts that Pilar could not take Maria away from him, that he and Maria are one, which prompts Pilar to muse that, when younger, she could have replaced Maria but that she now accepts the current situation. Pilar and Jordan are certainly integrated through conversation. Pilar evinces her need for this acceptance from Jordan in chapter nine when she says, "Everyone needs to talk to someone" (89). To Stanton and so many other scholars, Spanish characters serve as models regarding how to behave for Jordan, who more often than not is ready to accept, adapt, and integrate.

Stanton also turns to the relationship between Anselmo and Jordan to illustrate their ethnorelativism. He describes them as "a pair in harmony despite their differences" (154). Stanton notes how, after the two bond, their language, their pronoun usage becomes less formal, just as Pilar drops referring to Jordan as Inglés. We can see how integrated Anselmo and Jordan have become in chapter 23 when others in camp are thinking about executing those from the other side after the war, even mixing up who is what side. Anselmo and Jordan, though, are on the same ethical page. Hemingway writes, "'that we should win this war and shoot nobody,' Anselmo said. 'That we should govern justly and that all should participate in the benefits according as they have driven for them. And that those who have fought against us should be educated to see their error'" (285). Anselmo prefers prison and rehabilitation to killing, the former only a slight improvement from the rock bottom of denial, killing.

Jordan himself is not a perfect model, and, with tongue firmly planted in cheek, war is not conducive to integration. Jordan is sexist toward Maria in many ways, one of the most interesting to me being his refusal to allow her to have whiskey, but he may be at his ethnocentric low after Pablo steals key material with which to blow up the bridge, and he delivers a profanity-laced tirade on Spaniards. In another instance, Stanton, again, is useful, as he writes of Jordan making the guerrillas stick with the mission rather than loyally helping El Sordo, the other guerrilla leader in the mountains, one whom Jordan would be wise to model for his ethnorelative ways as when he brought the whiskey or with his acceptance of the most different of all individuals, Death. War, indeed, hits the bottom of Bennett's scale, killing being total denial. There must be denial to accomplish the mission. It is, to put it in Bennett's terms, an ethnocentric means toward a more ethnorelative end. Think the American Revolution or the Civil Rights Movement. Jordan muses on himself in Hemingway's third person: "So, now he was compelled to use these people whom he liked as you should use troops toward whom you have no feeling" (162). Jordan's imperialist voice comes out when he suggests a retreat to the mountains of Gredos after the mission, a defensive statement upsetting everyone by putting his hand in where he didn't belong. Jordan is further insensitive when he lapses into English when he is upset.

6. Robert Jordan and the DMIS

Relational detailing, in fact, seems to drop off in Hemingway's novel as the action picks up. The mission must prevail, sensitivity and civility be damned. And, what about that world after the victory over the fascists? Recall Anselmo and Jordan agreeing that the defeated will need to be rehabilitated. Karkov comments on forced integration. "All must be brought to a certain level of political development; all must know why they are fighting, and its importance. All must believe in the fight they are to make and all must accept discipline" (246). To make matters worse, guerrilla warfare, particularly, is not conducive to integration, for there is little or no integration with the people. As Hemingway puts it, "You did your job and cleared out" (135). Hemingway even allows a defensive authorial intrusion when the narrator criticizes El Sordo's typically Spanish and, in his eyes, lame goodbye wave.

In this novel, though, Hemingway manages to make the strongest voice one that cries for integration. Despite the obvious insensitivity of war, there is a sense of integration among soldiers, and Hemingway captures that. "You felt, in spite of all the bureaucracy and inefficiency and party strife, something that was like the feeling you expected to have and did not have when you made your first communion" (235). On this mission, Jordan experiences a sense of integration, of oneness with people very different than him. Jordan's previous experiences and the closeness with this one provides opportunity for Jordan's empathic growth. Bennett writes in *Basic Concepts*, "the more people from the other culture that we actually meet and empathize with the more specific our experience can become" (48). In the next sentence of the novel, the sensation of oneness is associated with experiencing music and architecture, and the whole point of this book is that literature is another art form that can facilitate that sense of oneness for an outsider to experience in a different cultural setting. Robert Jordan was an outsider and, granted the fighting enriched the integration, especially in the sense of fighting for all; however, Jordan also brings to the table skills, skills that can be learned, skills that enabled him to integrate in other ways, skills such as when he compliments Maria and Pilar describes him as one who talks "like the good ones" (65). It's enough to make one wonder why Edmund Wilson would characterize Robert Jordan as "detached" (32).

Most notably would be his strong language skills and his existential calm, the almost Taoist embracing of the spontaneity of life. Bennett writes in *Basic Concepts* of this carpe diem notion and how intercultural experience fosters such a notion, that dealing with difference creates a kind of existential focus on the work at hand, emphasizing living in the moment. An illustration of this kind of living in the moment can be found in these words from Jordan's mind, "So if life trades its seventy years for seventy hours I have that value now and I am lucky enough to know it. And if there is not any such thing as a long time, nor the rest of your lives, nor from now on, but there is only now, why then now is the thing to praise and I am very happy with it" (166). Jordan's existential focus on the now enhances his sensitivity. Underhill and Nakjavani clearly summarize the ethnorelative strides Jordan has made in this short life time, listing he's been initiated into the customs of the group, drunk their wine, eaten their authentic food, shared their struggle, and has even fallen in love with one of them (121). At this same point in the novel where Jordan is realizing what a rich life he has and has had, he begins translating "now" into several languages, then "night," then on to translating "life," "wife," "dead," and "war." Language skills would be at the top of Bennett's ethnorelative scale.

The ability to integrate through communication is critical, not simply in the sense of understanding the language of a host culture— Spain in this instance—but understanding language in the Benjamin Franklin sense of avoiding absolute diction and making word choices sensitive to differing points of view, a skill Jordan demonstrates with word choices such as "almost never." It is not surprising, then, to find that Jordan also dislikes the rigidity in the military's orders. He recognizes the sense in the sensitivity in language that has some wiggle room so that others of differing opinion are not minimized, denigrated, or denied their individuality. Recall Hemingway links certainty with bigotry, writing "To be bigoted you have to be absolutely sure that you are right" (164), a sense that also wouldn't play well with the more existential character of the novel. Further opposed to the damning sense of certainty that foils so much progress toward ethnorelative behavior, this openness that Hemingway emphasizes is yet another trait that binds Jordan with Anselmo. We see a similar sensitivity with language allowing for relational wiggle room when the old man thinks of atoning for killing. "Later on there may be certain days that one can work for the state or something that one can do that will remove it. It will probably be something that one pays as in the days of the Church" (198). The sensitive lack of rigidity here in Anselmo's creed resembles the Quaker striving to avoid a rigid creed by not writing it down.

Hemingway's novel, though, is quite instructive when it comes to analyzing characters on the opposite end of Bennett's relational scale because sometimes it is productive to understand something by what it is not, and this novel set during the Spanish Civil War is loaded with examples of Bennett's ethnocentric characteristics. Pablo, naturally, comes to mind first. His drunken berating of Jordan and American men as effeminate skirt wearers comes to mind specifically first. As in an earlier cave scene, it seems everyone wants Pablo dead, but Pablo also appears to be a master of Bennett's model. Jordan transforms Bennett's linear model into a wheel when he notes Pablo going so low in his treatment of others only to turn around and behave more relational. Pablo "pushes his hatred with insults to the point where you are ready to do away with him and when he sees that this point has been reached he drops it and starts all new and clean again" (222). Jordan later applies similar wheel imagery to the fluctuation of Karkov's levels of sensitivity. Pablo, though, at best, is moody.

Pablo, who is even dismissive to horses, is dismissive of Jordan much earlier in the narrative, not accepting the outsider, turning to Jordan when the conversation turns to alternative hideouts and asks, "What right have you, a foreigner, to come to me and tell me what I must do?" (15), a question that leads Jordan to wish he were born in Spain in what Bennett would describe as reverse minimization. Defensive in the derogatory nature of "a foreigner" and a denial of existence in the sense of having no rights, these words clearly place Pablo's position within the lower registers of Bennett's ethnocentric scale. So in Hemingway's novel we learn primarily what to do from Jordan and what not to do from Pablo. Stanton recognizes this, characterizing Pablo as culturally insensitive and uncivil (155–156). Pablo becomes a foil for Jordan, enabling readers to identify with any ethnocentric characteristics they may share with Pablo while also identifying with Jordan's more ethnorelative behavior. Robert A. Lee in 1983 wrote about how Jordan, during this initial crisis when Pablo verbalizes his ethnocentric position, adopts what Bennett would describe as a more relational path and "tries to negotiate his way through to Pablo's trust" (92). Pablo is not a lost soul, though.

Though Pablo's character ultimately bottoms out to the lowest level of Bennett's relational scale once Pilar tells the story of the massacre, there are some examples of even Pablo, this bloody killer, being more relational. For instance, he is, at least, relational, usually, with his environment, further opening the door for Bennett's DMIS to be applied to ecocriticism. But, for now, let's simply state that Pablo is integrated with his environment to the point that he knows that a snow will let up and that the skies will clear up. In his 2002 book, Robert Gajudusek even suggests a kind of sexual integration through Pablo's character, seeing Pilar become more manly and Pablo less manly, and as Pablo's character changes there is a kind of sexual reversal from the patriarchal to the matriarchal within the camp, reminiscent of Stephens' emphasis on the more magical mindset into which Jordan must integrate.

As briefly noted, before, Robert Jordan is also flawed, and the best example of his ethnocentric side is, again, regarding Pilar's palm reading. Pablo is not the only character in the novel from whom we can learn how to be by what not to do. Ian Hancock has written brilliantly on the abuse of Romani or gypsy characters in literature in his *We Are the Romani People* from 2002. David Murad hones that view in *For Whom the Bell Tolls*, particularly focusing on the palm reading. Pilar has noticed that Jordan's life line is short and refuses to share her reading with Jordan although her silence makes things pretty clear. For the most part, Pilar and Jordan exhibit strong relational skills on Bennett's scale; however, Murad points out that when Pilar is more like a gypsy, the connection is weak (98), yet when the two are relating about the mission, they seem more connected.

Analyzing the time after the awkwardness with the palm reading, Murad writes, "Shared communication and understanding return briefly when Robert Jordan tells her that he believes in 'work'" (99). Murad adds, "Robert Jordan 'likes,' or accepts [Pilar's] way of speaking in reference to the Spanish cause; but when they return to the subject of palm reading, Jordan no longer understands her. Misunderstanding then becomes frustration and anger" (99). War and sensitivity do not play well together.

Yet, *For Whom the Bell Tolls* is not limited to war when it comes to exemplifying insensitivity. The reference to the Ohio lynching in the novel is telling, for Hemingway witnessed such a thing in Ohio. The idea of being more accepting of difference is a large part of the novel. Critics and scholars for decades have been analyzing how Hemingway seems to address sensitivity and civility in the novel. In 1992, Mark Van Guten discussed how Hemingway's structure contributes to complexities of difference. Different storylines, "coupled with the stories Jordan's band share with one another, also reveal the overwhelming complexity of differing fighting units, differing political considerations and motivations, and differing experiences of the combatants on both sides" (146). It almost sounds like the alternating pattern of Jewett's *The Country of the Pointed Firs*, doesn't it? Van Guten recognizes the problem in relating to difference, and he has his solution that fits perfectly within the context of Bennett's DMIS and the behaviors of acceptance and adaptation that must replace ethnocentric behavior. Van Guten adds, "In order to interpret successfully, however, one must decenter the self from its restrictive egoism" (155). Van Guten's "restrictive egoism" is Bennett's ethnocentrism, and Hemingway's Robert Jordan is ethnorelative.

Others besides Van Guten have eloquently addressed this matter. Allen Josephs describes Robert Jordan as integrated, writing of his "knowing la Gloria; having felt the earth move; being selfless and giving completely of himself; accepting that he can have his whole life in seventy hours; believing now in the intuitive along with the rational, the female side of him and the male, the dark along with the light, feeling himself a part of humanity, bridged to John Donne's *Mankinde*; lying on the Spanish earth" (153). Robert Jordan is liminal. Todd Onderdonk in 2006 describes Jordan as "sensitive" (62), and Alex Link in 2009 turns, as so many other scholars have, to Jordan's relationship with Maria to discuss issues of sensitivity toward difference in the novel. Link notes how Jordan's name gets readers thinking about such things as rivers and bridges, barriers and links, and claims, "for Jordan, Maria embodies the seamless integration, or bridging, of contradictory values. That she does so in a novel written across cultures furthers the sense that the novel is replete with unbridgeable distances" (134–135). Still, other bridges are crossed.

For Whom the Bell Tolls may be about blowing up a bridge, but that symbolism walks in shadow under the gaze of Bennett's DMIS, a lens by which readers can gauge levels of sensitivity with characters, and using the model with Hemingway's novel turns out to be quite instructive, whether we are trying to avoid ethnocentric behavior or are modeling ethnorelative behavior, building bridges in other words. Hemingway's novel addresses complex expatriate issues and intercultural sensitivity. In her recent work on the role of world novels populated with expatriate outsiders trying to fit in, integrate, be ethnorelative if you will, Caren Irr argues "the world novel's relatively more political and institutional sensibility requires a recovery from the specific consumerist psychology of the expatriate" (663). Hemingway's writing often gives us that, for above the kind of information typically associated with tourism-oriented travelogues, Hemingway, for certain in *For Whom the Bell Tolls,* gives us a pattern for humanity to better relate to difference, and that is why I decided to focus on him for the last novel covered in this book.

Coda

A Practical Application to Prepare
Students for Study Abroad

But there is more to cover with Bennett's DMIS and literature, and in Cuba, and with ideal results, I have put into practice this theory of using literature to prepare students for accepting difference. Without attempting to completely detail the confusing history of United States/Cuba travel policy, let us start with the Bill Clinton administration in 1999, when academic travel to Cuba became a reality, temporarily, until the George W. Bush administration severely restricted such travel along with family visits in June 2004. The Obama administration revisited those Clinton-era Cuban travel standards, but with the addition of allowing for short term study-abroad trips to Cuba. Previously, such trips to Cuba had to be a semester, and this change fit well with my university's (Lynn University) newly developed January Term, or J Term, also known as a Winterim elsewhere, a two-and-a-half-week term after the holidays but before the start of spring semester. In January 2011, the idea of "Hemingway's Cuba," a Lynn J term academic program abroad, was born with sights on January 2012. John Daily, an English professor and published Hemingway scholar, Sheila Sheppard, a multilinguist specializing in study abroad, and I were the originators. We ultimately incorporated intercultural sensitivity theory that was primarily delivered through Ernest Hemingway's literature set in Cuba, effectively educating students about Hemingway's style and themes while simultaneously preparing them for cultural difference.

The plan fit well within Bennett's DMIS and his thinking as expressed in *Basic Concepts.* There are points Bennett makes regarding pre-departure activities to train students, and the method we employed follows his prescriptive writing. Bennett writes, "One way to focus on intercultural learning is to have programmatic elements that present frameworks for construing subjective cultural differences and that provide opportunities for exploring these differences" (118–119). As fortune would have it, much of Hemingway's style and themes match well with core Cuban values after the "triumph" of the Communist revolution. Thematically, two important levels of Hemingway's writings involve Marxism and existentialism. Stylistically, Hemingway's modernist tendencies, particularly his affinity for minimalism and stream of consciousness, link strongly with the Cuban way of life since Fidel Castro led the revolution against the dictatorship of Fulgencio Batista in January 1959. By covering these characteristics in Hemingway's literature pre-departure with readings and class discussions, we are educating students in these key Cuban concepts that will provide "a general respect for cultural difference and increased ability to adapt to cultural difference" (119). The literature became the framework creating the opportunity for students to accept these Socialist and existential values before experiencing them in Cuba, effectively decreasing the potential for an ethnocentric experience and increasing the odds of a more ethnorelative one.

Faculty Directors of Academic Programs Abroad (APA) would prefer to limit the potential for conflict caused by cultural insensitivity. Since, as Jaime Wurzel points out in his important 1988 anthology, "conflicts arise from not sharing cultural knowledge" (2), students need to somehow be exposed to the host culture of their APA before going abroad, which is difficult when embargos and other political posturing have been as prevalent as they have been between the United States and Cuba. Fortunately, three of Hemingway's novels could take us there: *To Have and Have Not, The Old Man and the Sea,* and *Islands in the Stream.* The economic themes in *To Have and Have Not* clearly synthesize with Communist Cuban economic policy. Santiago's grace under pressure in *The Old Man and the Sea* also echoes contemporary Cuban values and exemplifies the code hero embraced by Fidel Castro and Che Guevara. Thomas Hudson in *Islands in the Stream* further enriches a code hero whose existential and modernist characteristics also reflect the current Cuban character. Theoretically, the student who reads these Hemingway works will, at least, have some prior intercultural Cuban experience. In his equally important anthology from 1993, R. Michael Paige notes that experience almost always helps (9). Bennett adds in *Basic Concepts* that pre-departure course work "provides participants with schemata to organize their experience abroad" and makes them more "aware of how their own perspective may differ from that of the host culture" (121–22). Given that travel to Cuba has been so restricted, we had to, at first, travel there through Hemingway.

Our goal was to put our students into a position of acceptance, the first of Milton J. Bennett's ethnorelative stages, which, again, he marks with respect for behavioral difference and respect for value difference. Reading and discussing Hemingway's *To Have and Have Not,* his indictment of Capitalism, before traveling to Cuba made our students more accepting of, for example, the seeming disinterest in materialism, consumerism, and advertising evident in Marxist Cuba. Try to buy a camera there. After dropping mine, I did. It's impossible. Reading *The Old Man and the Sea,* the students could now be more accepting of the Cuban work ethic so grounded in existentialism and the code hero as well as help them envision Cojimar, where we will dine at La Terraza, above where old Santiago hauled in the skeletal remains of his great catch. Focusing on the "Cuba" section of *Islands in the Stream* advances the students' understanding of the code hero as well as setting up our students for visits to Hemingway's home, the Finca Vigía outside Havana, and haunts such as La Bodeguita del Medio and La Floridita. In another significant anthology in the field of study abroad, this one edited by Kenneth Cushner in 1998, the

Coda

editor himself warns those who have "a strong preference for interactions with similar others" (5) will run into conflicts in an APA. Using literature in conjunction with intercultural sensitivity theory affords the opportunity to address any such preferences and advance intercultural competence. Our mission simply became teaching these Hemingway novels with a focus on the themes and stylistic tendencies to help develop intercultural competence in Cuba.

Agreeing on what those themes and styles would be was easy: Marxism, existentialism, modernism, and the code hero. We just needed to make sure we were right about those being important aspects of Cuban culture. Assuming most of us are comfortable assigning Marxist as an adjective descriptive of post-revolution Cuba, even though Raul Castro and Miguel Diaz-Canel have recently initiated significant capitalist change, let us first, then, consider the Marxist existential character of this island. Jean-Paul Sartre noticed it right away. He visited the island at the dawn of the revolution and witnessed Cuba creating its own reality. Impressed by the work ethic of Fidel Castro and Che Guevara, their willingness to work hard against odds, their disdain for absolute truth and consequent embracing of flux and change, their drive to live in the moment, their disdain for abstraction, Sartre ultimately wrote a book, *Sartre on Cuba* (1961), about the characteristics of these charismatic leaders of what would ultimately become a Marxist revolution in Cuba. Sartre's book portrays two heroes trying to live by example amid the chaos and absurdities of a revolution. The French existentialist closes his book, observing that the work Cuba "does day after day under foreign pressure takes on, in its eyes, an original and profound meaning" (160). Early on in the revolution, Castro himself showed certain affinities to existential thinking. Sartre quotes Castro, "I say that if someone doesn't do all he can all the time—and more—it's exactly as if he did nothing at all" (123). Rather extreme at the end, but notice the affinity to Sartre, who writes in "The Humanism in Existentialism," an essay that goes by several other titles, "A man is involved in life, leaves his impress on it, and outside of that there is nothing" (48). And, how involved should man be? Furthering the connection, Sartre adds in the same definitive essay that man is not only "responsible for his own individuality, but that he is responsible for all men" (36). So, one of the principles of existentialism emphasizes this need to act, to work hard, and to be an example. Such characteristics link the character of Castro and Sartre in an existential bond.

The character of Che Guevara, whose visage, works, and words are almost ubiquitous in Cuba, also emphasizes this principle of work. In his essay "Socialism and Man in Cuba," addressing the time right after the revolution, Guevara adds, "This was the first heroic period, and in which combatants competed for the heaviest responsibilities, for the greatest dangers, with no other satisfaction than fulfilling a duty" (150). But one needs look no further than the famous architectural relief on the side of Cuba's Ministry of Interior building facing onto the Revolutionary Plaza in Havana. Under the relief of Guevara it reads *"Hasta la Victoria Siempre,"* or, literally, "Until the Victory Always." The notion of work is there. The notion of repetitive action with no end in sight is there. These key existential characteristics and more can be seen in Cuba and in the themes that present themselves in the literature of Hemingway.

Also in Hemingway's literature is a style, described as modernist by most. Within the umbrella of modernism and within the stylistic tendencies of Hemingway's writing is minimalism, which suggests less abstraction, less description, more of an impetus on the reader to become actively involved in the work of reading, and, at its base, simple sentence structures and simple vocabulary. This minimalist stylistic tendency in Hemingway fits right into what Guevara writes, again from "Socialism and Man in Cuba." Describing how work is initiated and performed, Guevara writes that Cubans are able to take the directive from on high but ultimately "make it their own" (151). This resounds with the existential concept of man creating his own reality, a sentiment which Castro states early on in his spoken autobiography with Ignacio Ramonet. "I made myself into a revolutionary" (23). In fact, in the early days of the revolution, when Manuel Urrutia was president, the bearded rebels from the Sierra Maestra seemed to recognize the drawbacks of abstraction and the power in clear, direct work aimed at improving the lot of humanity. Sartre's early observations of the revolution are again instructive when he points to Urrutia's inflexible principles, particularly when it came to brothels and casinos, and Castro's willingness to embrace, at the time, flux and change, sex and money. And, as for the notion of simplicity, Hemingway's style clearly reflects Cuban existentialism and its disdain for abstraction and embracing of the basic perspective of existence and work. As Sartre writes in "The Humanism of Existentialism," "I've got to limit myself to what I see" (47). He could just as well replace the first-person pronoun with "The Cuban." With Hemingway, what we see is what we get, and Cubans tend to likewise avoid abstraction, being a very realistic people.

Furthermore, Hemingway's modernist use of multiple points of view reveals the idea that the truth is unstable, which also fits into the existential idea of no fixed absolutes. With no fixed absolutes, the existentialist, or the Cuban, is able to create his own reality, without the influence of outside forces. Since "The Special Period," which is what the Cubans call their time after the departure of the Soviet influence, Cuba has been without a "sugar daddy." Whatever reality they are creating, it is their own. In fact, now more than ever, the existential character of the revolution can be linked to this concept of living in the moment, for Cuba has so many pressing needs, she finds herself like Dr. Rieux in Albert Camus' *The Plague*, constantly facing a critical situation, and there is almost always another critical situation so that what evolves is a series of moments. These experiences create a reservoir of memories, enabling the Cuban to almost intuitively respond to a bounty of certain given situations. As Leo Huberman and Paul Sweezy write in the *Monthly Review* in 1960, "A revolution is a process, not an event," unfolding "through many stages and phases. It never stands still. What is true of it today may be untrue tomorrow and vice versa" (77). This is like a living stream of consciousness, like the living reality of life in Cuba. This also reflects on Hemingway's social conscience in *To Have and Have Not*, the first text we studied prior to our departure.

Hemingway received criticism in the 1930s, during his Key West years, for not having enough of a social conscience in his literature. These arguments turned to the rather bourgeois character of such works as *Death in the Afternoon* and *Green Hills of Africa*, traveling to bullfights and going on safaris a bit out of the realm of the typical worker's experience. However, Hemingway's literature does have a social conscience, and his essay on the 1936 Labor Day Hurricane that struck Islamorada, Florida, in the Middle Keys, is a good example of it. More than 200 World War I veterans died, or as Hemingway puts it were left to die. They had been building a bridge so that the New Deal could come to Key West and transform this town that has, economically, lost so much: cigars to Tampa, sponges to Tarpon Springs, and its status as the major gulf port to New Orleans. This backdrop is significant because in "Who Murdered the Vets?" Hemingway lambasts the government for its neglect of the veterans; moreover, Key West is the setting for *To Have and Have Not*, and the New Deal is not welcome by the Conchs, the natives of Key West in the novel, which comes out a year after the hurricane. Hemingway lets a vet speak in the novel, "They've got to get rid of us. You can see that, can't you?" (206). It appears that it is not in the government's best interest to keep this particular segment of the population alive since they pose a threat to the potential capitalistic gain available for those in power.

The economic situation in 1930s Key West, whether real or imagined, is potent. As Albert, a fated mate in the novel explains, "They are only going to give us three days a week on relief now. I just heard about it this morning. I got to do something" (144). For Albert that means ultimately dying during a desperate attempt to make some money because the government, in the novel and in the hurricane essay, seems to be interested only in making money for itself and a select few. In both the essay and his novel, Hemingway's critique of savage Capitalism helps explain, in part, why he is still so venerated in Cuba. These works do have a social conscience, and while they do not embrace big government, they definitely criticize Capitalism.

Since Cubans are indoctrinated in school about savage Capitalism and are encouraged to develop their social consciences to the fullest, we chose to start our students with *To Have and Have Not*. We instructed them to read the book; then, we spent a two-hour class going over the novel, focusing on those aforementioned themes and stylistic tendencies. It was easy. The novel lends itself to just such an analysis. The title itself points to a bourgeois (the haves) and proletariat (the have-nots) conflict, and in this novel the haves are weak, seemingly unworthy of their position. One woman wants to buy Harry Morgan, the main character of the novel, like a pet. On an autobiographical level, and few are as autobiographical as Hemingway, this can be seen as a cut against his in-laws, the Pfeiffers, some particular artists, the government, and certainly certain tourists, but, viewed metaphorically, Cubans, and our students, can read this as a metaphor for Cuba's own struggle to create their own reality without Spain, the United States, or the Soviet Union treating them as a pet. The Cubans would be the have-nots while the various imperialists would be the haves.

Creating a kind of oppressor/oppressed situation, big government is not the answer in the novel, for Hemingway specifically targets Franklin Delano Roosevelt's New Deal as making matters worse. In 1934, Julius Stone was sent down as part of the Federal Emergency Relief Administration's effort to economically transform and, in the eyes of the government, save Key West. Stone created the Key West Administration and with an eye toward tourism dollars as the saving grace of the island, considered forcing Conchs to wear Bermuda shorts so that everyone would look in character, much like Disneyworld today. The Conchs in the novel, like the population they are based on, and Batista-era Cubans by metaphoric extension, live under a curfew and dislike the federal government's liberty-infringing efforts. The protagonist of the novel, Harry Morgan, especially follows this kind of code. Morgan, by the way, only has a left arm; additionally, his wife refers to him as a loggerhead, a threatened species. The figurative possibilities abound with such wording although the character seems to defy definitive labeling. Morgan is a kind of libertarian. He can't get ahead and blames outside forces. He wants more independence. He worries about money, urging his daughters to go swimming because it's free fun as opposed to going to the movies. He worries about feeding his family. Despite unease in labeling Morgan's politics, there is, at least, no denying the anticapitalist layer to the novel. This helps prepare our students for anticapitalist tendencies in Cuba, and when discussed in a context of Cuban history, we feel this approach definitely worked well for us.

A close reading of the novel provided numerous illustrations of our theme as almost every chapter of the novel addresses the notion of savage Capitalism and its negative effects on characters, especially Conchs who just want to be left alone to create their own reality, further cementing the novel as a helpful tool in preparing our students for existentialism in this study-abroad experience. Though he really only wants to make "honest money" (121), Morgan is tempted right away to take a risk and smuggle Chinese for good money, but this goes against his principles, and there's a risk he could lose his boat. How risky such entrepreneurship might be becomes clearer a few pages later when the principals involved in the smuggling have a shootout. Still, making a buck is seemingly just as difficult with his honest work chartering his boat for fishing. The rich man, Johnson, ends up stiffing Morgan for the large fee he owed our captain, who then finds himself broke and close to despair. This would be similar to the lesson of imperialism in Cuba, in which a few made big money while the many had to resort to almost any means to make ends meet, and Morgan finds himself breaking his code and resorting to smuggling Chinese. He is corrupted. He feels the system has left him no choice, something he repeatedly laments later in the novel. Soon, he is receiving threats for the business he has chosen. A little later, he kills. This is what savage Capitalism can lead to.

In fact, Morgan loses his arm in a smuggling job, one that goes awry with a shootout that leaves Morgan's shot Black mate left to ask, "Ain't a man's life worth more than a load of liquor?" (69). As fate would have it, a federal man, probably linked to Stone, comes upon Morgan's shot up boat and thinks he has an opportunity to strut his authority; however, the Conch captain of the boat, Willie, keeps the federal man from coming down with all of his authority on Morgan, pulling away and saying, "If he wanted us he would have signaled us. If he don't want us it's none of our business. Down here everybody aims to mind their own business" (79). The Fed can only see Morgan as a lawbreaker, but Captain Willie, Morgan's friend, knows more of the truth, knows that the government plays a part in causing this bloodshed because the government is corrupt, aiming to hypocritically capitalize where it can. Captain Willie questions as they pull away from Morgan's shot up boat, "Ain't you mixed up in the prices of things that we eat or something? Ain't that it? Making them more costly or something. Making the grits cost more and the grunts less?" (69). In addition to exposing Hemingway's social conscience, the passage is insightful when it comes to Cuba's history in which imperialist forces have forced Cuba's indigenous economy to become almost worthless while raising the cost of living.

The blending of Marxism and existentialism has become quite clear by this point in the novel, and we took advantage of the points in the novel where the syntheses occur, pointing them out to students so that they better understand how both the themes work in the novel and how the characteristics associated with those themes help expose them to their upcoming Cuban experience. When Johnson, for example, haggles with Morgan about how captains take the money even if the client doesn't catch any fish, almost always coming up with some reasonable excuse, Morgan affirms that is indeed the way it is and that there's not much one can do about it. Here, we have both a conflict within the capitalistic transaction and the awareness of human limitations, Morgan hammering home a sense of existential futility by adding, "Then when you get a day that's perfect you're ashore without a party" (14). In a chapter that Albert narrates, he has a conversation with Morgan that further evinces this bond between Marxism and existentialism in the novel. Neither man can explain the absurd situation in which they find themselves. They want to work but cannot find any, and Morgan turns the talk toward that savage Capitalism with "what they're trying to do is starve you Conchs out of here so they can burn down the shacks and put up apartments and make this a tourist town" (96). In the next chapter, switching the narrative voice to Harry, yet another example resounds with the possibilities of educating students about two revolutionary Cuban characteristics in one when Morgan laments that he has no choice, that the corrupt government has put him in this position, and that he must do what needs to be done.

The switching of these voices is equally significant for our attempts to create cultural competence through literature, and Hemingway's inventive use of voice here is indicative of his modernist style in literature. We often think of William Faulkner and James Joyce, but Hemingway, too, was at the vanguard of this style, and in *To Have and Have Not* we are able to focus on this style and link it to yet another existential characteristic, one which revolutionary Cubans would be quite accustomed to, multiple perspectives of the truth, rendering the truth ambiguous. Making our students more accustomed to traits such as this helped put them in an early position to accept cultural difference, having had the exposure through our analysis of the novel, which begins in Part One with first-person narration from Morgan but doesn't stay there, moving to third person in Part Two, and different voices in Part Three. These latter are the chapters with Albert and Morgan speaking before this part moves back into third person. The multiple voices suggest multiple truths, breaking down the concept of fixed absolutes and further cementing the literature and Cuban existential character that thrives on creating its own reality.

In addition to these multiple voices, Hemingway employs another modernist technique. His emphasis on using the right word helps illustrate his disdain for abstraction and his interest in clear, concrete reality. After years of imperialism, Cuban culture also has a disdain for abstraction and an interest in clear, concrete reality. So, when we point out when Morgan corrects Mr. Sing, who has just used the word *accommodate* in reference to smuggling while Morgan prefers "carry" (32), we are putting our students into a better position to accept and adapt to the Cuban host culture. The above example also evinces Hemingway's minimalist tendencies, which additionally can be seen when his third-person narrator in Part Two understatedly sums up the pretty wretched, shot-up condition of Morgan and his mate after running into trouble on a liquor run with simply "things were bad" (71). They were much worse than that, but this tendency to understate works well on a similar level as seen before with the characteristics of abstraction and reality, and Hemingway utilizes this move with some frequency, notably when he refrains from revealing the full details of an upcoming trip to his wife, Marie, preferring to leave the matter with "I'm going on a bad trip" (127). Such a technique also plays into the existential notion of the reader creating his own reality from the narrative since the narrator is leaving matters rather up in the air.

Hemingway's modernism, though, is not limited to minimalistic evidence, for in addition to his multiple perspectives, he also likes to try to abandon perspective and slip into a stream of consciousness with the third person revealing what a character is thinking, usually ending with a "he thought," as at the end of such a stream of modernism at the beginning of chapter eight, or a "she was thinking" at the start of such a stream (114). Hemingway's use of stream of consciousness clearly connects to the current Cuban value system. On an existential level, the stream of consciousness technique suggests the notion of living in the moment. The narrative comes unedited, without outside censorship, as a pure pouring forth of the instantaneous thoughts of the narrator. This links back to the code hero and living in the moment. In *To Have and Have Not*, this is clearly seen when the narrator reveals that Morgan has two moves to make near the start of chapter 16, two moves being rather minimal, but they are also a part of his code of behavior.

The other two novels also help continue this sensitivity training. *The Old Man and the Sea* especially reinforces the existential Cuban character and the code hero. Much has been written on this quality in Hemingway's novel. We all know about Santiago's seemingly futile quest, his winner take nothing mindset, his poor results from great effort, but, at this point, instead of retreading over those instances from that novel or from *Islands in the Stream*, let us gather dear reader that you get it, that letting literature prepare students for study abroad helps them better relate. Other novels by other writers could provide similar insights for those about to embark to settings in those novels.

Conclusion

In the year before the Treaty of Paris was signed in 1783, recognizing the independence of the United States of America, a Frenchman, Michel-Guilluame-Jean de Crèvecoeur, under the pseudonym J. Hector St. John, sold a series of his essays to a London bookseller, who published them as *Letters from an American Farmer*. Letter III, entitled "What Is an American," presents the first characterization of the United States as a melting pot. Crèvecoeur writes, "Here individuals of all nations are melted into a new race of men" (598) and for over a century after those words were written the metaphor appears to have been somewhat accurate. Robert Ward, in a 1924 article in *Foreign Affairs*, explains that during most of that first century, "The number of immigrants was still very small, and nearly all of them were sturdy pioneers, essentially homogenous and readily assimilated. There was, therefore, little need to worry about any immigration 'problems'" (100). However, at the end of the nineteenth century, that was all about to change, and for most of the twentieth-century sociologists, anthropologists, and politicians continually wrestled with the metaphor of the melting pot.

Nobody more clearly explains how America maintained a melting pot for as long as it did than another Frenchman, Alexis de Tocqueville. In his landmark, two-volume *Democracy in America*,

Conclusion

he points out that despite differences, early American immigrants united. Here is the ethnorelative behavior marking the upper echelon of Bennett's Developmental Model for Intercultural Sensitivity. For the most part, common language, poverty and misfortune, democratic pasts, strong independent values, and a large middle class all lent themselves to a general equality among early immigrants. But the melting pot was maintained for only so long, and many of de Tocqueville's factors conducive to the melting pot ultimately herald its fall. For example, in the first volume of his great work de Tocqueville calls America's unifying independent spirit a kind of "township independence" (42), which becomes threatened with the rise of a more urban, materialistic society. Also, that same independent spirit translates into an individual spirit that promotes flux, and the two, flux and independence, feed off of each other like fire and gasoline, resulting in frequent movement of individuals within classes, which, in and of itself may seem conducive to maintaining a melting pot, particularly because of the way de Tocqueville further advances his point in the second volume where he writes that when "each class gradually approaches others and mingles with them, its members become undifferentiated and lose their class identity for each other" (105). This theorizes that Bennett's integration, if carried out for a long enough period of time, could turn everyone into the people in the gray jump suits in all the B science fiction films I grew up on.

However, before we would get to that point, something could alter this integration from becoming the homogenous, almost fascist, civilization of my nightmares. All this movement creates upward mobility and a kind of Capitalism that leads to the breakdown of family units, causing members of families to leave their family unit and seek their piece of the American Dream, a cultural tendency that may be incongruent with the values of immigrants from less democratic and more family-based cultures, which is true of recent American immigration trends. So, at this point there is a clear conflict between values within a capitalistic culture. The melting pot theory points to one side becoming dominant. See, even the theory is insensitive. Furthermore, a melting pot becomes a precarious thing when the gap between the haves and the have-nots becomes wide and the gap between theories on the true corrective course becomes even wider. Add to the old melting pot immigrants who do not speak English, which only becomes a significant factor because also added are those who bring significantly different customs, who do not have an equal education, and who are segregated, and the oppression that results from all of this truly threatens the melting pot. Melt or else.

To be sure, at the end of the nineteenth-century, the United States was no longer a melting pot. Capitalism won out. Certain insensitive words were in vernacular vogue, words like *nativism*, stemming from fears toward Native Americans and freed slaves, and *nationalism*, stemming from labor disputes and job shortages and used to justify the fall of Native Americans. U.S. imperialism and Capitalism brought a lot of this division on. As Joan London writes, "Wage slaves were wanted now, not Americans. And so the melting pot, which had served the country well in the past, gradually ceased to function" (qtd. in Baym et al. 1147). Some, such as Jack London's daughter, civically engaged for change while others began to stew over the fall of the melting pot. Frederick Jackson Turner turned to the West in a desperate search for the new melting pot, and Theodore Roosevelt chastised immigrants who stuck to their Old World ways, claiming this practice was harmful to both the immigrant and America. For the ole Rough Rider, assimilation was necessary and must be promoted.

In 1909, one of the most blatant literary attempts to promote assimilation occurs; Israel Zangwill's play *The Melting Pot: Drama in Four Acts* appears. Zangwill's play is clearly influenced by the social settlements, mini-melting pots, that sprung up at the turn of the century in the U.S., most notably among them in Chicago with Jane Adams' Hull House, which bridges time and space through, for instance, clothes making by Syrian, Greek, Italian, Russian, and Irish women all huddled together in a settlement. Her writings also illustrate the power of compassion and empathy in creating a kind of unity. Zangwill's play has its settlements, too. Vera, the heroine of the drama, runs a settlement with Dutchmen, Greeks, Poles, Norwegians, Welsh, and Armenians all getting along nicely. Zangwill's main drive, though, is to present Jewish assimilation as a model

Conclusion

meant to rebuke anti-Semitism. Jewish characters in the play read classic American texts, sacrifice the Sabbath to be an American and work, and they even forget certain Jewish holidays. The play's two protagonists, a Jewish man (David) and a Christian woman (Vera), ultimately fall in love and come to represent the unifying force of the melting pot. In his penultimate speech, David calls America the melting pot and adds, "There gapes her mouth [He points east]—the harbour where a thousand mammoth feeders come from the ends of the world to pour in their human freight. Ah, what a stirring and a seething! Celt and Latin, Slave and Teuton, Greek and Syrian—black and yellow" (184). The play had a certain amount of popularity.

However, even at the time of Zangwill's play, immigration patterns in the United States were affecting the metaphor of the melting pot, and a series of late nineteenth-century and early twentieth-century acts limiting Asian immigration such as the Immigration Act of 1924 all recognize the effort toward limiting immigration in order to preserve the melting pot, which is simply seen as a way of promoting and maintaining one culture, in essence denying all others and subsequently scoring low on Bennett's scale because this is not now simply a theory but a mindset. The immigration acts didn't work.

In fact, within the same year of the Immigration Act of 1924, Horace Kallen's book of essays entitled *Cultural Pluralism* appeared, and by the end of the 1960s, with the bare facts from the U.S. Bureau of the Census pointing to the decline of the old homogenous population of the country and with the publication of Nathan Glazer and Daniel Moynihan's *Beyond the Melting Pot,* most researchers recognized that the cultural deficit model of the melting pot had in fact been replaced by a cultural difference model, something clearly more in line with Bennett's DMIS. Milton M. Gordon's 1964 *Assimilation in American Life* points out that "American society has come to be composed of a number of pots" (130). Consequently, a new metaphor was needed to explain what an American is. Bicultural models ultimately gave way to more pluralistic metaphors such as a goulash or a tossed salad. However, writers such as Jules Chametzky argue that there never has been a melting pot, nor is there currently a tossed salad or goulash. Instead, what an American is has always been in flux. Glazer and Moynihan's seminal text points toward this notion, suggesting that "the American nationality is still forming; its processes are mysterious, and the final form, if there is ever to be a final form, is as yet unknown" (315).

Two relatively recent attempts from around the turn of the last century try to define the American, a simple thing to do for Crèvecour, and show the individual difference and the flux that de Tocqueville once presented as a unifying force. Here, we see how far apart we are when defining an American. In his 1993 book, *A Different Mirror: A History of Multicultural America*, Ronald Takaki seems to dispute there ever was a melting pot and argues that America has always been racially diverse. Still, he sees unity when he writes, "On their voyage through history, Americans have found themselves bound to each other, especially as workers" (426). He presents California as the new social model of America because the state shows a significant demographic change, the majority no longer descending from White Europeans. On the other hand, Samuel P. Huntington recognizes the storied tradition of the old model, the original melting pot, and warns of the effects from its demise. In his 2004 book, *Who Are We? The Challenges to America's National Identity*, Huntington claims, as his title suggests, that immigration without assimilation is a problem.

More recently, scholarly journals have revisited the enduring vision of Glazer and Moynihan's book showing the flux of American society. In spring 2000, *The International Migration Review* ran an issue featuring a series of essays celebrating 35 years since the initial publication of Glazer and Moynihan's *Beyond the Melting Pot*. Philip Kasinitz' article "Beyond the Melting Pot: The Contemporary Relevance of a Classic?" uses diction such as the fusion chamber in describing New York as "a cauldron that seems constantly on low simmer. But it rarely boils over in the ways we have seen in Los Angeles and Miami" (254). Among the other contributors to the special edition of *IMR* is Nathan Glazer himself, whose most telling line is "We no longer have markedly dominant immigrant groups" in New York City (272). Writing the introduction for the special edition was

Conclusion

Richard Alba, who has been writing about the United States becoming more racially diverse since the last millennium with important articles on rethinking assimilation and multiculturalism. A recent work comes from summer 2019. Alba writes an essay for another edition focusing on the significance of Glazer and Moynihan's book, this time in *City and Community*. In it, Alba writes, "notions of assimilation today have been forced to take the differentiation [*Beyond the Melting Pot*] depicted into account" (448). Again, note the emphasis on difference.

Research continues to point toward the need to follow the upper stages of Bennett's DMIS: acceptance, adaptation, and integration. Take for instance this 2013 journal article from *Teaching in Higher Education*. The authors, Andrea Balis and Michael Aman, ask whether such sensitivity can be taught. As history and theater/film professors, Balis and Aman early on in their essay turn to Ernest Morell, whose important 2002 work posits, "Popular culture can help students deconstruct dominant narratives" (72). The answer is yes, and Bennett's DMIS provides a way for us to organize our analysis of whatever it is we happen to be studying in the culture, American novels for instance, for the purpose of becoming more sensitive to difference. By studying these American novels under the gaze of Milton Bennett's DMIS, students at least develop a cultural self-awareness, and Bennett affirms in *Basic* Concepts "host-culture learning should constantly be integrated with own-culture learning" (121). For Balis and Aman, the title of the essay was the title of their class. The relational focus of the class was race. They chose to begin class readings with Harriet Beecher Stowe's *Uncle Tom's Cabin*. That's the beauty of literature. The conflicts in narrative can take a reader right to action in which characters must, for instance, accept or deny difference, exhibiting a predominant experience within the objective world of an American novel. Balis and Aman write, "We discovered that messiness is a necessity in a discussion of race" (588). They ultimately embraced the conflict in the texts and films they presented to their students, something this book supports.

There are so many possibilities with Milton Bennett's DMIS and its application to literary analysis. I was recently rereading *The*

Hunchback of Notre Dame and came to the conclusion that Esmeralda was one of Bennett's liminal characters. Victor Hugo characterizes her as very relational, quite open to accept difference, having traveled abundantly. From her varied experience, she has "gathered scraps of strange tongues, queer song and notions, which made her conversation as motley a piece of patchwork as her dress, half Parisian and half African. Moreover, the people of those quarters of the town which she frequented, loved her for her gaiety, her gracefulness, her lively ways, her dances, and her songs" (246–247). When Quasimodo suffers, it is Esmeralda alone who has the compassion to relate to him, accept him. She is Hugo's model of relational living. And, if I cannot travel like Esmeralda, at least, I can travel in my mind and read works of great literature. Every country has within its canon a literature that addresses the idea of the outsider trying to fit in, the accepting of difference. It is a major conflict.

One can easily imagine books of contemporary literature helping people relate to different cultures. Reading about different cultures enables the reader to be in a position to more readily accept difference, not be surprised by it, whether a different culture has entered the neighborhood, or whether travel takes one to a different culture. We can take Bennett's theory along the way across contemporary literature from any country and create helpful guidebooks to prepare people for a more relational integrative life rather than one characterized by walls and ethnocentrism. Frederick C. Corey and Catherine T. Motoyama, two contemporary proponents of mimetic theory, write, "Literature is a source of information about the individual and the culture" (77). From ecocriticism and beyond, intercultural sensitivity theory can certainly enhance our understanding of how literature provides us with models to make the world a better place.

This book isn't trying to expunge incivility. It couldn't do it. But it may help decrease incivility caused by not relating to difference. Hopefully, these American novels by some of our greatest writers have addressed this topic, especially under the gaze of Milton Bennett's DMIS, and shed some light on how easily relational behavior can be tracked. One who denies the existence of another, solely

Conclusion

because that other is different, would ideally be moved by similar characters who progress toward being more relational, a progress not unlike Charles Darwin's evolutionary process in which species that adapt survive, and as we have seen throughout this book, those who exhibit relational behavior can often thrive.

For now, though, study abroad seems like the logical place to start. The lessons of intercultural sensitivity may not be limited to cultures. However, for our focus, consider what some of the top scholars in the field say is important about cultural sensitivity training, keeping in mind that following Melville's characterization of Ishmael may very well be revealing the ideal trainer. To be sure, intercultural sensitivity helps lead to intercultural competence (Hammer, Bennett, and Wiseman 422), and Ishmael's competence, as well as the competence evinced by other characters in these six American novels, is again best seen in the ability to combine disparate ways of thinking. Anderson et al. ask, "Are there activities that students should participate in prior to participation in a study abroad program that would significantly enrich their overseas experience and lead to greater intercultural sensitivity?" (46–47). Yes, a literature class designed with an eye toward intercultural sensitivity would be a snap.

Bibliography

Alba, Richard. "Beyond the Melting Pot." *City and Community* 18.2 (June 2019): 446–450.

Alba, Richard, and Victor Nee. *Remaking the American Mainstream: Assimilation and Contemporary Immigration.* Cambridge: Harvard UP, 2003.

Ammons, Elizabeth. *Conflicting Stories: American Women Writers at the Turn into the Century.* New York: Oxford UP, 1991.

Anderson, Philip H., et al. "Short Term Study Abroad and Intercultural Sensitivity: A Pilot Study." *International Journal of Intercultural Relations* 30.4 (2006): 466–67.

Armengol, Joseph M. "Race Relations in Black and White: Visual Impairment as Racial-ized and Gendered Metaphor in Ralph Ellison's *Invisible Man* and Herman Melville's *Benito Cereno. Atlantis* 39.2 (2017): 29–46.

Ashwill, Mark A. "Developing Intercultural Competence for the Masses." *International Educator* 13.2 (Spring 2004): 16–25.

Balis, Andrea, and Michael Aman. "The Race Race: Assimilation in America." *Teaching in Higher Education* 18.6 (2013): 587–595.

Baym, Nina. "Revisiting Hawthorne's Feminism." *Nathaniel Hawthorne Review* 30.2 (2004): 32–55.

Baym, Nina, et al. "Debates Over 'Americanization.'" *The Norton Anthology of American Literature, Vol. C.* New York: Norton, 2012, 1147–1148.

Bender, Geoff. "'I Feel a Giddy Sickness of Pain': Chillingworth, Cenci, and the Silent Pleasure of Pain." *Nathaniel Hawthorne Review* 42.1 (Spring 2016): 56–72.

Bennett, Janet M. "Cultural Marginality: Identity Issues in Intercultural Training." *Education for the Intercultural Experience.* Ed. R. Michael Paige. Yarmouth, ME: Intercultural, 1993, 109–135.

Bennett, Milton J. *Basic Concepts of Intercultural Communication: Paradigms, Princi-ples, and Practices.* 2nd ed. Boston: Intercultural Press, 2013.

_____. "Becoming Interculturally Competent." *Toward Multiculturalism: A Reader in Multicultural Education.* Ed. Jaime Wurzel. Newton, MA: Intercultural Resource, 2004, 62–77.

_____. "Towards Ethnorelativism: A Developmental Model of Intercultural Sensitiv-ity." *Education for the Intercultural Experience.* Ed. R. Michael Paige. Yarmouth, ME: Intercultural, 1993, 21–71.

Bibliography

Bercovitch, Sacvan. *The Office of The Scarlet Letter.* Baltimore: Johns Hopkins UP, 1991.

Brown, Merlin. *The Long Encounter: Self and Experience in the Writings of Herman Melville.* Chicago: U of Chicago P, 1960.

Bryant, John. "Democracy, Being, and the Art of Becoming America." *College English* 59.6 (Oct. 1997): 705–711.

Callahan, John. *In the African-American Grain: The Pursuit of Voice in Twentieth Century Black Fiction.* Urbana: U of Illinois P, 1988.

Castro, Fidel, and Ignacio Ramonet. *Fidel Castro, My Life: A Spoken Autobiography.* New York: Scribner, 2009. Print.

Chametzky, Jules. "Beyond Melting Pots, Cultural Pluralism, Ethnicity: Or, Déjà Vu All over Again." *MELUS* 16.4 (Winter 1989–90): 3–17.

Chase, Richard. *The American Novel and Its Tradition.* Garden City, NY: Doubleday, 1957.

Corey, Frederick C., and Catherine T. Motoyama. "Toward Cultural Awareness through the Performance of Literary Texts." *MELUS* 16.4 (Winter 1989–90): 75–86.

Crèvecoeur, J. Hector St. John de. "Letters from an American Farmer, Letter III: What Is an American." *The Norton Anthology of American Literature, Vol. A.* Ed. Nina Baym et al. New York: Norton, 2012, 596–616.

Crews, Frederick C. "Introduction." *Great Short Works of Nathaniel Hawthorne.* Ed. Frederick C. Crews. New York: Harper, 1967, vii--xii.

Cushner, Kenneth. "Intercultural Education from an International Perspective: An Introduction." *International Perspectives on Intercultural Education.* Ed. Kenneth Cushner. Mahwah, NJ: Erlbaum, 1998, 1–13.

_____. "Intercultural Education from an International Perspective: Commonalities and Future Prospects." *International Perspectives on Intercultural Education.* Ed. Kenneth Cushner. Mahweh, NJ: Erlbaum, 1998, 353–370.

Davis, Arthur P. "Integration and Race Literature." *Black Voices: An Anthology of Afro-American Literature.* Ed. Abraham Chapman. New York: Mentor Books, 1968.

de Montainge, Michel. "On the Cannibals." *Selected Essays.* Ed./Trans. Stanley Applebaum. Mineola, NY: Dover, 2007, 118–143.

de Tocqueville, Alexis. *Democracy in America.* Vols. 1 and 2. New York: Vintage, 1945.

"DMIS." *The International Encyclopedia of Intercultural Communication.* Ed. Young Yun Kim. Hoboken, NJ: Wiley-Blackwell, 2018, 643–652.

Donne, John. "Meditation 17." *The Norton Anthology of English Literature: Major Authors,* 6th ed. Ed. M. H. Abrams. New York: Norton, 1990.

Donovan, Josephine. "Sarah Orne Jewett's Critical Theory: Notes toward a Feminine Literary Mode." *Critical Essays on Sarah Orne Jewett.* Ed. Gwen L. Nagel. Boston: Hall, 1984, 212–225.

Dumm, Thomas L. "Who Is Ishmael?" *Massachusetts Review* 46.3 (Sept. 2005): 398–414.

Dupee, F. W. *Henry James.* New York: Sloane, 1951.

Eagleton, Terry. *Literary Theory: An Introduction.* Minneapolis: U of Minnesota P, 1983.

Edel, Leon. *Henry James: A Life.* New York: Harper, 1985.

Egan, Philip J. "Time and Ishmael's Character in 'The Town-Ho's Story' of *Moby-Dick*." *Studies in the Novel* 14.4 (Winter 82): 337–347.

Ellison, Ralph. *Invisible Man.* New York: Vintage, 1972.

Fiedler, Leslie A. *Love and Death in the American Novel.* New York: Criterion, 1960.

Finnerty, Páraic. "Celebrities of the Future: Fame and Notability in Henry James's *Roderick Hudson* and *The American.*" *Critical Survey* 27.3 (2015): 24–42.

Folsom, Marcia McClintock. "'Tact Is a Kind of Mind Reading': Empathic Style in Sarah Orne Jewett's *The Country of the Pointed Firs.*" *Critical Essays on Sarah Orne Jewett.* Ed. Gwen L. Nagel. Boston: Hall, 1984, 76–89.

Gajdusek, Robert E. *Hemingway in His Own Country.* Notre Dame: U of Notre Dame P, 2002.

Bibliography

Geller, Allen. "An Interview with Ralph Ellison." *Tamarack Review* 32 (1964): 3–24.

Gillman, Susan. "Regionalism and Nationalism in Jewett's *Country of the Pointed Firs.*" *New Essays on* The Country of the Pointed Firs. Ed. June Howard. Cambridge: Cambridge UP, 1994, 101–117.

Glazer, Nathan. "On Beyond the Melting Pot, 35 Years After." *International Migration Review.* 34.1 (Spring 2000): 270–279.

Glazer, Nathan, and Daniel Patrick Moynihan. *Beyond the Melting Pot.* 2nd ed. Cambridge: MIT P, 1970.

Gordon, Milton M. *Assimilation in American Life: The Role of Race, Religion, and National Origins.* Oxford: Oxford UP, 1964.

Guevara, Ernesto Che. "Socialism and Man in Cuba." *Manifesto: Three Classic Essays on How to Change the World.* Melbourne: Oceans, 2005, 147–168. Print.

Hammer, Mitchell R., Milton J. Bennett, and Richard Wiseman. "Measuring Intercultural Sensitivity: The Intercultural Development Inventory." *International Journal of International Relations* 27 (2003): 421–443.

Hancock, Ian. *We Are the Romani People.* Hatfield: U of Hertfordshire P, 2002.

Hawthorne, Nathaniel. *The Scarlet Letter* in *The Great Short Works of Nathaniel Hawthorne.* Ed. Frederick C. Crews. New York: Harper, 1967.

Hemingway, Ernest. *For Whom the Bell Tolls.* New York: Scribner, 1995.

_____. *Islands in the Stream.* New York: Scribner, 1970. Print.

_____. "Letter to Maxwell Perkins, Feb. 7, 1939." In Carlos Baker, *Ernest Hemingway Selected Letters 1917–1961.* New York: Scribner, 1981. Print.

_____. "Letter to Pauline's Sister, Nov. 12, 1926." In Carlos Baker, *Ernest Hemingway Selected Letters 1917–1961.* New York: Scribner, 1981. Print.

_____. *The Old Man and the Sea.* New York: Scribner, 1996. Print.

_____. *To Have and Have Not.* New York: Scribner, 2003. Print.

Hirsch, David H. "Notes: Melville's Ishmaelite." *AN&Q* 5.8 (Apr. 1967): 115–116.

Huberman, Leo, and Paul Sweezy. *Cuba: Anatomy of a Revolution.* New York: Monthly Review, 1960.

Hugo, Victor. *The Hunchback of Notre Dame.* New York: Barnes & Noble, 2008.

Huntington, Samuel P. *Who Are We?: The Challenges to America's National Identity.* New York: Simon & Schuster, 2004.

Irr, Caren. "Toward the World Novel: Genre Shifts in Twenty-First Century Expatriate Fiction." *American Literary History* 23.3 (2011): 660–679.

Italia, Paul G. "Henry James's *The American*: The House of Bellegarde and The House of Atreus." *CLA Journal* 42.3 (March 1999): 364–369.

Jackson, Holly. "'So We Die before Our Own Eyes': Willful Sterility in *The Country of the Pointed Firs.*" *The New England Quarterly* 82.2 (2009): 264–284.

James, Henry. *The American.* New York: Penguin, 1986.

Jewett, Sarah Orne. *The Country of the Pointed Firs.* Ed. Jeff Morgan. Lewiston, NY: Mellen, 2003.

Josephs, Allen. *For Whom the Bell Tolls: Ernest Hemingway's Undiscovered Country.* New York: Twayne, 1994.

Kalter, Susan. "A Student of Savage Thought: The Ecological Ethic in *Moby-Dick* and Its Grounding in Native American Ideologies." *ESQ: A Journal of the American Renaissance* 48.1–2 (2002): 1–40.

Kasinitz, Philip. "Beyond the Melting Pot: The Contemporary Relevance of a Classic?" *International Migration Review* 34.1 (Spring 2000): 248–255.

Kierkegaard, Søren. *Either/Or. Vol. II.* Trans. Walter Lowrie. Rev. Howard A. Johnson. New York: Anchor, 1959.

Kilcup, Karen. "Sarah Orne Jewett's *The Country of the Pointed Firs.*" *American Writers: Classics.* Ed. Jay Parini. New York: Scribner, 2002, 67–88.

Knutson, Susan Lyne. "Bowering and Melville on Benjamin's Wharf: A Look at

141

Bibliography

Indigenous-English Communication Strategies." *Essays on Canadian Writing* 38 (Summer 1989): 67–80.

Lee, Robert A. "'Everything Completely Knit Up': Seeing *For Whom the Bell Tolls* Whole." *Ernest Hemingway: New Critical Essays.* Ed. Robert A. Lee. London: Vision, 1983, 79–102.

Lesser, Simon O. *Fiction and the Unconscious.* Chicago: U of Chicago P, 1975.

Lhamon, W. T. *Deliberate Speed: The Origins of a Cultural Style in the American 1950s.* Washington, DC: Smithsonian, 1990.

Link, Alex. "Rabbit at the Riverside: Names and Impossible Crossings in Hemingway's *For Whom the Bell Tolls.*" *Hemingway Review* 29.1 (Fall 2009): 134–139.

Littenberg, Marcia. "From Transcendentalism to Ecofeminism: Celia Thaxter and Sarah Orne Jewett's Island Views Revisited." *Jewett and Her Contemporaries: Reshaping the Canon.* Ed. Karen Kilcup and Thomas S. Edwards. Gainesville: UP of Florida, 1999. 137–152.

Long, Robert Emmet. *Henry James: The Early Novels.* Boston: Twayne, 1983.

Magowan, Robin. "The Outer Island Sequence in *Pointed Firs.*" *Colby Library Quarterly* (June 1964): 418–429.

Marx, Leo. *The Machine in the Garden: Technology and the Pastoral Ideal in America.* London: Free Association, 1991.

Matthiessen, F. O. *American Renaissance: Art and Expression in the Age of Emerson and Whitman.* Oxford: Oxford UP, 1941.

McElderry, Bruce R. *Henry James.* New York: Twayne, 1965.

McGregor, Ian M., Alan S. Marcus, and David M. Moss. "Promoting Intercultural Competence in Professional Spaces: Education Abroad Experiences in England for Social Studies Preservice Teachers." *Global Education Review* 6.4 (2019): 31–49.

Melville, Herman. *Moby-Dick, or The Whale.* New York: Penguin, 2001.

Millichap, Joseph. "Fiction, Photography, and Cultural Construction of Racial Identity in Ralph Ellison's *Invisible Man.*" *South Atlantic Review* 76.4 (Fall 2011): 129–142.

Morell, Ernest. "Toward a Critical Pedagogy of Popular Culture: Literacy Development Among Urban Youth." *Journal of Adolescent and Adult Literacy* 46.1 (2002): 72–77.

Morris, Ruth. "U.S. Latino Population Could Triple by 2050." *South Florida Sun-Sentinel*, February 12, 2008, 1A+.

Murad, David. "The Conflict of Being Gypsy in *For Whom the Bell Tolls.*" *Hemingway Review* 28.2 (Spring 2009): 87–104.

Onderdonk, Todd. "'Bitched': Feminization, Identity, and the Hemingwayesque in *The Sun Also Rises.*" *Twentieth-Century Literature* 52.1 (Spring 2006): 61–91.

Ostendorf, Berndt. "Anthropology, Modernism, and Jazz." *Modern Critical Views: Ralph Ellison.* Ed. Harold Bloom. New York: Chelsea, 1986, 145–172.

Paige, R. Michael. "On the Nature of Intercultural Experiences and Intercultural Education." *Education for the Intercultural Experience.* Ed. R. Michael Paige. Yarmouth, ME: Intercultural, 1993, 1–19. Print.

_____. "Trainer Competencies for International and Intercultural Programs." *Education for the Intercultural Experience.* Ed. R. Michael Paige. Yarmouth, ME: Intercultural, 1993, 167–199.

Paige, R. Michael, et al. "Assessing Intercultural Sensitivity: An Empirical Analysis of the Hammer and Bennett Intercultural Development Inventory." *International Journal of Intercultural Relations* 27 (2003): 467–486.

Paterson, Mark E. "Democratic Leadership and Narrative Authority in *Moby-Dick.*" *Studies in the Novel* 16.3 (Fall 1984): 288–303.

Poirier, Richard. "*The American* and *Washington Square*: The Comic Sense." *Henry James: Modern Critical Views.* Ed. Harold Bloom. Chelsea: New York, 1987.

Reising, Russell. *The Unusable Past: Theory and the Study of American Literature.* New York: Methuen, 1986. Print.

Bibliography

Rosenblatt, Roger. *Black Fiction.* Cambridge: Harvard UP, 1974.

Sartre, Jean Paul. "The Humanism of Existentialism." *Essays in Existentialism.* Ed. Wade Baskin. Trans. Bernard Frechtman. New York: Citadel, 1993, 31–62. Print.

_____. *Sartre on Cuba.* New York: Ballantine, 1961. Print.

Schultz, Elizabeth. "Melville's Environmental Vision in *Moby-Dick*." *Interdisciplinary Studies in Literature and Environment* 7.1 (2000): 97–113.

Scott, Nathan A. "Ellison's Vision of Communitas." *Ralph Ellison's Invisible Man: A Casebook.* Ed. John F. Callahan. Oxford: Oxford UP, 2004, 109–124.

Shulman, Robert. "Community, Perception, and the Development of Stephen Crane: From the Red Badge to 'The Open Boat.'" *American Literature* 50.3 (1978): 441–460.

Stanton, Edward F. *Hemingway and Spain: A Pursuit.* Seattle: U of Washington P, 1989.

Steinem, Gloria. "Testimony Before Senate Hearings on the Equal Rights Amendment (6 May 1970)." *Voices of Democracy.* https://voicesofdemocracy.umd.edu.steinem-testimony-speech-text/.

Stephens, Robert O. "Language Magic and Reality in *For Whom the Bell Tolls*." *Criticism* 14.2 (1972): 151–164.

Strychacz, Thomas. "The Kitchen Economics of Sarah Orne Jewett's *The Country of the Pointed Firs*." *Legacy: A Journal of American Women Writers* 32.1 (2015): 53–74.

Takaki, Ronald T. *A Different Mirror: A History of Multicultural America.* Boston: Little-Brown, 1993.

Tanner, Tony. "The Music of Invisibility." *Modern Critical Views: Ralph Ellison.* Ed. Harold Bloom. New York: Chelsea, 1986, 37–50.

Turner, Victor. *The Ritual Process: Structure and Anti-Structure.* New York: de Gruyter, 1969.

Underhill, Linda, and Jeanne Nakjavani. "Food as an Element of the Iceberg Principle." *Readings on Ernest Hemingway.* Ed. Katie de Koster. San Diego: Greenhaven, 1997, 114–122.

Van Gennep, Arnold. *The Rites of Passage.* Chicago: U of Chicago P, 1960.

Van Guten, Mark C. "Polemics of Narrative & Difference." *Blowing the Bridge.* Ed. Rena Sanderson. New York: Greenwood, 1992, 143–157.

Ward, Robert. "Our New Immigration Policy." *Foreign Affairs* 3.1 (Sept. 1924): 99–110.

Weber, Donald. "Outsiders and Greenhorns: Christopher Newman in the Old World, David Levinsky in the New." *American Literature* 67.4 (Dec. 1995): 725–745.

Wiesel. Elie. "Elie Wiesel: The Perils of Indifference." *American Rhetoric.* https://www.americanrhetoric.com/speeches.ewieselperilsofindifference.html (original speech April 12, 1999).

Williams, Stanley T. "Some Spanish Influences on American Fiction: Mark Twain to Willa Cather." *Hispania* 36.2 (May 1953): 133–136.

Wilson, Edmund. "Hemingway: Gauge of Morale." *Modern Critical Views: Ernest Hemingway.* Ed. Harold Bloom. New York: Chelsea, 1985, 17–33.

Wright, John S. "Dedicated Dreamer, Consecrated Acts: Shadowing Ellison." *Carleton Miscellany* 18.3 (1980): 142–199.

Wurzel, Jaime S. "Multiculturalism and Multicultural Education." *Toward Multiculturalism: A Reader in Multicultural Education.* Ed. Jaime S. Wurzel. Yarmouth, ME: Intercultural, 1988, 1–13. Print.

Young, Philip. *Ernest Hemingway: A Reconsideration.* University Park: Penn State UP, 1966.

Zangwill, Israel. *The Melting Pot: Drama in Four Acts.* New York: Macmillan, 1915.

Zoellner, Robert. *The Salt-Sea Mastodon: A Reading of Moby-Dick.* Berkeley: U of California P, 1973.

Index

145

Index

146

Index

Shakespeare, William: Hamlet 16; Romeo and Juliet 66
socialism/communism 89, 92, 98, 106, 110, 120–121, 123
Socrates 105
Spain 9, 29, 88, 105–118, 126
Steinem, Gloria 12
Stevens, Wallace 102

Tao 105, 114
Theocritus 52
Thoreau, Henry David 33, 45
transcendentalism 26, 33, 89
Turgenev, Ivan 62
Turner, Frederick Jackson 133

Turner, Victor 8–10, 96, 100–101
Twain, Mark 97

Uncle Tom 101, 136

Van Gennep, Arnold 8–9, 52, 60, 102, 108
Veronese, Paolo 72

Washington, Booker T. 98
Washington, George 23
Whitman, Walt 15, 91, 102
World War I 125
World War II 94

Yale 25

www.ingramcontent.com/pod-product-compliance
Lightning Source LLC
Chambersburg PA
CBHW050613280326
41932CB00016B/3025